MISSOURI 365

This Day in State History

John W. Brown

Library of Congress Control Number: 2021935138

ISBN: 9781681063294

Cover design: Eric Marquard
Interior design: Linda Eckels

Cover images are courtesy of the Springfield CVB, Elms Hotel & Spa/Hilton, Bass Pro Shops/Big Cedar Golf, the Missouri State Archives, the Library of Congress, or are believed to be in the public domain. Interior images are courtesy of the author or believed to be in the public domain unless otherwise noted.

Printed in the United States of America
21 22 23 24 25   5 4 3 2 1

Contents

Introduction

Missouri seems to be right in the middle of everything. And that is true in nearly every sense of the word. We are right in the middle of the country, with the center of the United States population sitting in our state. We were the 24th state admitted to the Union thanks to the Missouri Compromise, which put us right in the middle of the U.S. Civil War. For decades, we were known as the "bellweather state" because Missourian voted for the eventual presidential winner in most every election in our history. Nearly every poll, survey, and national ranking seems to find the Show Me State right in the middle of the pack on everything. So it may surprise people that our average-sized state (21st largest) with an average sized population (18th most populous) would generate so much news of national interest. It seems that every week there is some event in Missouri that makes headlines across the country, or around the globe. As a reporter, I became fascinated when putting this book together. I combed through online sources, old newspapers, and even the class "microfilm" archives at several libraries to find the daily news stories that populate this book

Even though I have spent my career covering the news, mostly in Missouri, I was even shocked to find so many of these stories that changed the course of history. Many of the daily headlines were easy to choose (i.e. Dewey Defeats Truman), while other dates had several big stories to choose from. And there were three dates in particular where I had to dig and dig to find a story, although I won't tell you which dates they were. One thing that was frustrating was that so many online sources had the wrong dates, which were then copies by other sources. Several times I had to rework portions of the book because after finding the original source, I discovered that the dates published online were wrong. But that's what makes the news business so interesting.

In the process of verifying information, you discover news things you never knew.

So, I hope you find this book as fascinating to read as I did to write. There are events when you will remember exactly where you were the moment you heard the news. There are other events that I never realized had a Missouri connection. But one thing is for sure, if there is something big happening in America, you don't have to look very hard to find that a Missourian often had a connection to it.

JAN 01 — 2000: Missourians survive the Y2K (Year 2000) scare.

Millions of anxious people around the state waited to see if electronics would shut down at the stroke of midnight on January 1, 2000. Businesses and governmental agencies across the globe were concerned that systems would crash because programmers designed early software with two-digit date codes. The fear was that computers would recognize "00" as 1900, not 2000, and all personal and business records might be erased.

However, on New Year's Day everything was working correctly after hundreds of millions of dollars were spent making sure systems were Y2K-compliant.

JAN 02 — 1932: The Young Brothers Massacre.

The worst mass killing of law enforcement officers in the 20th century happened in Brookline (near Republic) when six police officers were gunned down by members of the Young family. Paul, Harry, and Jennings Young were small-time thieves who had spent time in prison, but they were back on the streets committing crimes. Law enforcement learned that two of the brothers were at their farmstead in southwest Missouri, so they went to question them about a recent murder. A shoot-out ensued, resulting in the deaths of the six officers as the brothers escaped. The two were eventually trapped in Texas, where they shot each other in a suicide pact.[1,2]

JAN 03 — 1851: The exact northern border of Missouri is established.

The border issue with Iowa was finally resolved by the US Supreme Court after years of disputes, including the "Honey War."

Missouri, Iowa border marker

The controversy originated with sloppy surveys commissioned by the United States government in 1816 and conducted by John Sullivan. The Sullivan Line defined which states were "Northern" and which were "Southern." That was especially important when it came to treaties and slavery issues, so Missouri had it re-surveyed in 1837. The two states could not reach an agreement over the disputed territory, which nearly led to bloodshed in the Honey War of 1839, so named because of trees being cut down in the disputed area that contained beehives. The border was eventually re-surveyed in 1851, and cast-iron markers were put in place to mark the boundaries along the official new border between Missouri and Iowa.[3, 4]

JAN 04 — 1932: The original "Uncle Sam" dies in Excelsior Springs.

The name of Frank Coburn may not be widely known, even though he was perhaps the most famous face in America during World War I. Coburn was originally from California and posed for pictures as Uncle Sam for decades. He crisscrossed the country in that role and eventually landed in Missouri. He checked into the US Veterans' Hospital in Excelsior Springs in 1931 and died a year later. Uncle Sam is buried in Crown Hill Cemetery outside of the town.[5]

Springfield, courtesy of State Historical Society of Missouri

JAN 05 **1835: Springfield is named the Greene County seat of government.**

The irony of the decision by the state legislature was that Springfield wasn't even an incorporated town at this point and hadn't had an official survey. John P. Campbell arrived in the area in 1829 to set up a home for his family. By the time the legislature decided to make it the county seat, there were only about two dozen log cabins in the wide-open countryside. Springfield wasn't officially incorporated until 1838, when Campbell laid out the town's grid on 50 acres of land that were deeded to set up the county seat.[6]

JAN 06 **1963: Mutual of Omaha's *Wild Kingdom* debuts.**

Marlin Perkins became a household name across America, thanks to the popularity of his wildlife show. Perkins was born in Carthage, educated at Wentworth Military Academy in Lexington, and later studied at Mizzou. He began his career at the Saint Louis Zoo, left for a few years, then later returned as the zoo's director. But from 1963 to 1988, he was the star of *Wild Kingdom*, where he and the show won multiple Emmy Awards and recognition for their conservation efforts.[7]

JAN 07

1962: Police raid G. E. M. Department stores and arrest 70 employees for doing business on Sunday.

G.E.M. Membership Department Stores was a chain of department stores in the 1960s and '70s, much like Sam's and Costco of today. The issue was Missouri's Blue Laws, which prohibited certain types of commerce from taking place on Sundays. The case eventually went all the way to the Missouri Supreme Court in 1964, where the G. E. M. Southway Corporation argued that the Missouri law was unconstitutional and unenforceable because it targeted only specific types of businesses. The court upheld the Sunday sales laws, although Blue Laws were later repealed in Missouri.[8]

JAN 08

1894: Ralston Purina is founded as Robinson-Danforth Commission Company.

William Danforth opened a small feed store near the St. Louis riverfront in 1894; the company became Ralston Purina in 1902. The company traced its early growth to animal foods that included the name "Chow" and became a household name when they introduced breakfast cereals. The iconic Checkerboard Square symbolizes Danforth's key life concepts of balance in all four areas of life: physical, mental, social, and religious.[9, 10]

Academic Hall ruins

JAN 09 1892: Fire engulfs Academic Hall on the campus of Mizzou.

The massive blaze destroyed the original building on the campus of the University of Missouri-Columbia, leaving behind the six iconic columns as the only things standing. Many people wanted the columns to be toppled, but Mizzou Alumni Association President Gardiner Lathrop made a plea for them to remain. The president of the Board of Curators at the time, Gideon Rothwell, was moved by Lathrop's passionate appeal and stated, "Let the columns stand. Let them stand for a thousand years." The classical columns are now among the most emblematic symbols of Missouri.[11]

JAN 10 1945: Ozark Air Lines begins service around Missouri.

The first scheduled flights for Ozark Air Lines shuttled passengers between Springfield and St. Louis with the goal of connecting underserved communities in the Ozarks. The first iteration of the airline was short-lived due to political and logistical issues and shuttered two years after launching. Service was restored on September 26, 1950, and eventually connected towns across the state with cities throughout the Midwest. Ozark Air Lines was eventually bought out by Trans World Airlines in 1986.[12]

1822: The Great Seal of the State of Missouri is adopted.

Shortly after the State of Missouri was established, state leaders set out a plan to design a symbol that would encompass all the things that made the state special.

In the center of the seal is the United States' coat-of-arms with a bald eagle on one side and a crescent moon above a grizzly bear on the other. Surrounding the inner circle are the words, "United We Stand, Divided We Fall."

Outside the circle, two bears symbolize the state's strength and the bravery of its people. Below is a scroll of the official state motto, "Salus Populi Suprema Lex Esto," which means "Let the welfare of the people be the supreme law."

A helmet to represent state sovereignty sits atop the inner circle, which is just below a bright star surrounded by 23 smaller stars to represent the 23 other states that existed when Missouri became a state.

One other interesting fact about the seal is the Roman numeral MDCCCXX, or 1820, near the bottom. 1820 is the year Missouri began operations as a state, although statehood was established the following year, in 1821.[13]

2014: Southwest Airlines flight mistakenly lands at wrong airport in Branson.

The pilots of the Southwest 737 made a huge mistake when they landed at a small runway about seven miles from their intended destination. Although Flight 4013 from Chicago Midway was supposed to touch down at the new Branson Airport, it landed instead at the tiny College of the Ozarks Airport, which had only a 3,738-foot runway—about half the length that the pilots expected. Passengers had little idea that something was amiss until the plane filled with smoke as the jet's tires were locked up. The runway was so short the jet was not able to take off again, so its 124 passengers had to take a bus to the intended airport.[14]

JAN
1997 **12**

Steve Fossett takes off from Busch Stadium in the hot air balloon, "Solo Spirit"; Fossett set a world distance record when he landed in India.

JAN 13 — 1969: Warren E. Hearnes is sworn in as Missouri's 46th governor.

Warren Eastman Hearnes was born into extreme poverty in Mississippi County, but he rose through the political ranks to become

Governor Hearnes

the first governor in Missouri to serve two consecutive terms and the first governor in Missouri history to serve in all three branches of government. Hearnes grew up in Charleston, which he called home the rest of his life, even while working in Jefferson City. He served as a state representative, the secretary of state, and ultimately governor. The Hearnes Center on the Mizzou campus is named in his honor.[15]

JAN 14 — 1868: The only typewriter in the United States is being used in a courtroom in St. Louis.

The first typewriters looked nothing like what you would see today, but there were revolutionary for the time. In fact, the device didn't even have a name when the inventors in Milwaukee came up with it. But Charles Weller, a shorthand court reporter in St. Louis and acquaintance of inventor Christopher Latham Sholes, knew there was a demand for a machine that could help court reporters churn out hundreds of pages of legal drafts quickly, so he ended up testing the first machine. Later improvements were made by inventors Sholes and fellow inventors Carlos Glidden and Samuel Soule, and the typewriter soon became an office staple. Weller went on to write the book, The Early History of the Typewriter. [16]

JAN 15 — 1967: The Kansas City Chiefs play in the first-ever Super Bowl.

The Chiefs moved to Kansas City from Dallas in 1963 and found themselves in the championship game a few years later. The Chiefs won the AFL (American Football League), while the mighty Green Bay Packers won the NFL, making Super Bowl I a showcase between the leagues' two best teams. Even though Green Bay won the game 35-10, Kansas City was in the record books as part of that historic game.[17]

JAN 1953 15

Harry S. Truman becomes the first president in history to deliver his farewell address to the country via radio and TV.

JAN 16 — 1919: Prohibition is ratified, going into effect one year and a day later.

Prohibition had an impact on nearly everyone in America, although the impact in Missouri was greater than in most states. The Show-Me State was home to dozens of breweries and wineries prior to Prohibition, many of which didn't survive the 13 years during which the law was in effect. In St. Louis alone, there were at least 20 breweries operating in 1919, but only two were still in business when Prohibition ended—Falstaff and Busch. Kansas City was an anomaly in that the city largely refused to recognize Prohibition as a law, due in part to the power of political boss Tom Pendergast. On April 7, 1933, the Cullen-Harrison Act was signed legalizing beer with a 3.2-percent alcohol content. On that day, Anheuser-Busch sent President Franklin D. Roosevelt a case of Budweiser to commemorate the event.[18] Prohibition was repealed completely on Dec. 5, 1933.

Anheuser Busch plant

JAN 17 — 1952: Birthday of Joplin-born Darrell Porter, who was an MVP for both the Royals and the Cardinals.

There are only a handful of players who have played for both Major League Baseball (MLB) teams in the Show-Me State, and even fewer who were raised in Missouri. Darrell Porter is one of those few. Porter grew up in Joplin and landed with the 1976 Kansas City Royals, where he played until 1980, when he was traded to the St. Louis Cardinals. He had the unique honor of playing in the World Series for both Missouri teams, and was honored as the World Series MVP in 1982, setting him apart from all the other players who have ever played with both sides of the Interstate-70 rivalry.[19]

> Other Missouri natives to play with Cardinals and Royals (or Kansas City's previous American League team, the Athletics):
>
> **Cloyd Boyer,** Alba High School
> **Scott Cooper,** Pattonville High School
> **Mark Littell,** Gideon High School
> **Kerry Robinson,** Hazelwood Central High School
> **Trevor Rosenthal,** Lee's Summit West High School

JAN 18 — 1808: William Ray is born.

The name of William Ray may not be recognizable to most people, although the bustling town on the outskirts of Kansas City named in his honor sure is. Ray moved to Jackson County, Missouri, from Ohio to open a blacksmith shop along the Santa Fe Trail at a point where several additional trails also crossed, making it an early hub of commerce. His shop became so well-known as the area around Kansas City grew that locals began to refer to that area as "Ray's Town," even though there wasn't much of a town there at all. Eventually, the area officially became Raytown, which is now a bustling city of around 30,000 residents.[20]

JAN 19

2001: "Born to Fly" hits number one for Sara Evans.

The central Missouri native hit number one for the first time with the song, "Born to Fly," which also earned Evans her first Country Music Awards win (Video of the Year.) It was a huge beginning for the small-town girl from New Franklin. Since then, her albums have also won her numerous awards, including Female Vocalist of the Year from *Radio and Records* in 2006, Top Female Vocalist by the Academy of Country Music, and many more. She also made an appearance on ABC's *Dancing with the Stars* in 2006.[21]

JAN 20

1872: Governor Benjamin Gratz Brown moves into the newly completed Governor's Mansion.

The Missouri Governor's Mansion was built in 1871 as the third governor's mansion in Missouri history. The current mansion overlooking the Missouri River was built after many lawmakers said they would not dare come visit its predecessor because it wasn't safe. So, the state hired architect George Ingham Barnett to design the Neo-Renaissance structure. The elaborate mansion has since been refurbished several times, most recently by First Lady Teresa Parson in 2019. It was added to the US National Register of Historic Places on May 21, 1969.[22]

JAN 2006 20

The debut of *High School Musical* had young people dancing and made Lucas Grabeel of Springfield a star. The Kickapoo High alum starred in the most commercially successful Disney Channel Original Movie of all time.

Governor's Mansion, Jefferson City, Missouri

JAN 21 — 1826: Final meeting of the Missouri General Assembly in St. Charles.

St. Charles ended its run as the temporary seat of government for the state of Missouri as lawmakers wrapped up business and packed their belongings for the trip to Jefferson City. Early state leaders didn't want St. Louis to have too much political power because it was already the center of government for the Upper Louisiana Territory, but there were few other towns that could handle a delegation of legislators. Thanks to available space and one of the few established roads, the Boonslick Road, St. Charles was chosen to play host until a capitol was built in the newly established "City of Jefferson" being laid out in mid-Missouri.

First state capitol

JAN 22 — 1955: *Ozark Jubilee* begins a six-year run on national television.

Springfield was vying to dethrone Nashville as the Country Music Capital when entertainment executives launched a national TV show from the Ozarks. Red Foley was hired to host the *Ozark Jubilee* from the Jewell Theater near Park Central Square in downtown Springfield. The show was the first nationally syndicated country music show and was a launching pad for numerous stars. The inevitable end came in 1960 when the show ceased production, following charges against Foley for income tax evasion, of which he was later cleared.[23]

JAN 23

1986: Chuck Berry is among the first group of performers inducted into Rock and Roll Hall of Fame.

When the Rock and Roll Hall of Fame opened its doors in Cleveland in 1986, its first class consisted of the stars who music historians considered the best of the best.

In that class was St. Louis native Chuck Berry. He rose to fame with "Maybelline" in 1955 and stayed in the public eye for decades. Also in that first class were the likes of Elvis Presley, Ray Charles, and Jerry Lee Lewis.[24]

Other Missourians in the Rock and Roll Hall of Fame:

Michael McDonald (Doobie Brothers)

Tina Turner

Gene Clark (The Byrds)

Johnnie Johnson

JAN 24

1968: Powell Hall converts from a movie theater to a symphony hall.

The St. Louis Symphony Orchestra played its first-ever concert on the night after the legendary theater was converted. Powell Hall was formerly known as St. Louis Theater, but was renamed for local businessman Walter Powell when his widow donated $1 million for it to be refurbished as the home for the symphony. The ornate movie theater opened in 1925 with over 4,000 seats and showcased not only films but also live performances. The final film shown at the theater was the *The Sound of Music*, before the big screen came down in 1966.[25]

JAN 1922 24

The patent is granted to Russell Stover for the Eskimo Pie ice cream bar. The treat helped propel growth for Stover's company, Russell Stover Candies, which moved its headquarters to Kansas City in 1931.

JAN 25 1999: Bill Bradley kicks off his campaign for president.

One of Missouri's most famous sons threw his hat into the ring to seek the Democratic nomination for president against frontrunner Al Gore. The Crystal City native was a strong early contender but conceded the race to Gore months later. Bradley first rose to national prominence as a star basketball player. He won a gold medal in the 1964 Olympic Games in Tokyo before a successful NBA career with the New York Knicks, where he won two championships. He was inducted into the NBA Hall of Fame in 1982.[26]

JAN 1955 25

H&R Block is founded in Kansas City by Richard and Henry Bloch. Their small tax preparation firm went on to become one of the largest accounting firms in the world.

JAN 26 1999: Pope John Paul II comes to St. Louis.

One of the most famous guests in St. Louis history touched down at Lambert Airport for a 31-hour visit. Pope John Paul II was even greeted by President Bill Clinton as he stepped off the papal jet. Thousands of people packed the streets to see his motorcade as the Pope rode toward downtown St. Louis. He later held a youth rally with 21,000 young people at the Kiel Center

Pope John Paul II visits St. Louis, courtesy Getty Images

and then celebrated Mass with more than 100,000 at the Trans World Dome. The temperature on the second day of his January visit reached 68 degrees, which the Pink Sisters of Mount Grace Convent say they prayed for.[27]

1825: Congress approves the creation of the Indian Territory.

A tragic episode in American history was set into motion with this vote by Congress, supported by President Andrew Jackson. The creation of the Indian Territory in Oklahoma and Arkansas paved the way for the Indian Removal Act of 1830 and forced the relocation of Native Americans along what became known as the Trail of Tears. The Northern Route of the trail in Missouri began where the tribes crossed the Mississippi River, east of Jackson. They trudged through the rugged terrain toward present-day Rolla, then walked on a path toward Springfield, then toward

the Arkansas border. Other Cherokee tribe members branched off the Northern Route near present-day Ironton in the Arcadia Valley and took what is known as the Hildebrand Route. The other route through Missouri was further south and entered Arkansas near Doniphan. Tens of thousands of Native Americans died while walking the 5,043 miles of the Trail of Tears.[28]

1978: A deadly fire kills 20 in Kansas City.

A massive fire broke out at the Coates House Hotel in Kansas City, killing 20 people and making it one of the deadliest fires in Missouri history. The Coates House had fallen into disrepair at the time of the fire after once being a magnificent structure on Broadway and was inhabited primarily by transients and low-income residents. The hotel had gone through several changes since first constructed in 1886 on the land once owned by Kersey Coates who helped develop the upscale Quality Hill neighborhood. The hotel was eventually brought back to life in 1987 as up-scale residences.[29]

JAN 29

1944: The USS *Missouri* is christened.

The most famous battleship ever built was the third ship to be named after the state of Missouri. The "Mighty Mo" was christened by Mary Margaret Truman, President Truman's daughter. The ship took center stage during World War II on September 2, 1945, when General Douglas MacArthur and the Japanese delegation signed the Instruments of Surrender, officially ending the war. The ship has been retired twice and is now stationed in Pearl Harbor, where it stands as a museum and memorial.[30]

JAN 30

2000: St. Louis Rams win Super Bowl XXXIV.

One of the most exciting Super Bowls of all time ends with the Rams' Mike Jones making a tackle as time ran out, allowing St. Louis to defeat the Tennessee Titans 23-16. The victory was the culmination of an exciting season that nobody predicted. It started with the rise of quarterback Kurt Warner, who earned the starting job after an injury and led the team to a record-setting season in which they earned the nickname, "The Greatest Show on Turf."[31]

JAN 31

1929: The Fabulous Fox Theatre opens in St. Louis.

The Fox Theatre opened in 1929 with the showing of the film, *Street Angel*. When it opened, the elaborate structure was the envy of the world. The movie mogul behind the theater, William Fox, promised the city something special when he announced the construction of The Fabulous Fox in 1927, and he certainly delivered. At the time of its opening, the 4,500-capacity venue was the second-largest theater in America, and certainly one of the most ornate. Over the years, it transitioned from a movie theater, to a more traditional performance theater, showcasing some of the most famous performers from around the world.[32]

FEBRUARY

FEB 01 2004: Nelly performs at the Super Bowl XXXVIII halftime show.

Cornell Hanes Jr., aka Nelly, was on top of the world in the early 2000s after the success of his albums *Country Grammar* in 2000 and *Nellyville* in 2002. The University City native seemed to be everywhere, wearing shirts that represented his hometown teams, so it only seemed logical that he would be one of the headlining acts for the most-watched TV program of the year. Nelly performed his hit song, "Hot in Herre," alongside other big stars. But his performance ended up being largely forgotten when the final act showcasing Justin Timberlake and Janet Jackson ended with the infamous "wardrobe malfunction" that became talk-show fodder for weeks after.[33]

FEB 02 2020: Kansas City Chiefs win Super Bowl LIV.

Fifty years after their previous appearance in the Super Bowl, the Chiefs were crowned champions. The Chiefs defeated the San Francisco 49ers in Miami, Florida 31–20 after a furious fourth-quarter comeback. 24-year-old Patrick Mahomes was named the Super Bowl MVP by leading the team to 21 points in the final 6:13 of the game. Football fans in Missouri will also never forget the moments after the Chiefs won the AFC Championship on January 19, 2020 against the Tennessee Titans. Clark Hunt, whose family owns the Chiefs, accepted the Lamar Hunt Trophy, which was named in honor of his father, who co-founded the AFL and brought the Chiefs to Kansas City.[34]

FEB 1931 02 Lake of the Ozarks begins to fill after completion of Bagnell Dam.[35]

FEB 03 — 2004: Voters in Rockaway Beach approve gambling in their city.

Residents in the once-thriving resort town along Lake Taneycomo voted to allow riverboat gambling in hopes of reviving the town's economy. Despite local approval of a riverboat casino on the dammed White River, the measure still depended on a statewide vote. The problem was the state constitution only allowed gambling on the Mississippi and Missouri rivers, and the number of casino licenses was capped at 13. Introducing gambling to Rockaway Beach would have required a constitutional change, which Missouri voters rejected with 55.9 percent of the vote in August 2004.[36]

FEB 04 — 1893: Marble Cave gets national exposure on cover of *Scientific American* magazine.

The massive cave complex that sits below what is now Silver Dollar City is a geological wonder. The Osage Indians found the cave as early as the 1500s, but never went in because they feared what was inside, even naming it "Devil's Den." It wasn't until 350 years later, when geologists finally lowered themselves 200 feet into the main chamber, that the cave began to be explored more fully. The cave first got exposure in the *Scientific American* in 1885, then again on the cover of the same magazine's 1893 issue, "The Marble Cave of Missouri." That nationwide publicity made it a tourist attraction. Missouri's deepest known cave has a grand cavern so large that promoters inflated hot air balloons inside to showcase the size of the natural wonder.[37]

Marvel Cave, once known as Marble Cave

Old State Capitol

FEB 05 — 1911: The second Missouri State Capitol is destroyed by fire.

A bolt of lightning hit the dome of the Missouri State Capitol, sparking a fire that tore through the building. Firefighters from across mid-Missouri rushed to Jefferson City to try and save the building. By the time the sun came up and onlookers could survey the damage, the beautiful structure was a complete loss. The first state capitol in Jefferson City had also burned to the ground, back in 1837. The third capitol building to be erected, which is the current Capitol, took 6 years to build and opened in 1917.[38]

FEB 06 — 1959: Jefferson City native Jack Kilby files a patent for a "Miniaturized Electronic Circuit."

Kilby was one of the most prolific inventors in modern history, but his miniaturized electronic circuit changed all our lives. That invention paved the way for all future computer design and operation. He was an early employee of Texas Instruments, and his ability to process information helped him solve what was known as the "tyranny of numbers," which was holding back technology at the time. Kilby is also credited as the co-inventor of handheld calculators.[39]

Laura Wilder

FEB 07 — 1867: Birthday of Laura Ingalls Wilder.

Although Wilder was born in Wisconsin, she lived much of her life near Mansfield, where she wrote many of her famous books, including the *Little House on the Prairie* series. The Wilder family's move to the farmstead in Missouri in 1894 shaped the way she viewed life and changed the way we experienced pioneer life through her books and ultimately the TV series of the same name. Interestingly, she didn't even begin writing the series until she was 65. She spent the rest of her life at Rocky Ridge Farm until she died in 1957 at the age of 90.[40]

FEB 08 — 1853: The first planned suburban community west of the Mississippi is established.

The suburbs were born in Missouri when state lawmakers approved the incorporation of the "Kirkwood Association." Many residents of St. Louis were looking to move out of the city following the cholera outbreak and the Great Fire of 1849, and this pristine area 15 miles west of town along the Missouri Pacific Railroad offered them fresh air and more space to raise growing families.[41]

FEB 1947 08

The first TV station begins broadcasting in St. Louis. KSD was one of only 13 TV stations operating across the country at the time.

FEB 09

1844: Missouri's Governor commits suicide after breakfast.

Forty-seven-year-old Governor Thomas Reynolds had the outward appearance of an up-and-coming politician. The Kentucky native had already served in the Illinois legislature and as chief justice of the Illinois Supreme Court before moving to Fayette, Missouri, where he established a successful law practice and served as the Speaker of the Missouri House. He won the Missouri governor's office in 1840 and was to all appearances successful. But poor mental health took its toll, along with the constant criticism of elected office, and he shut himself inside his office in the Governor's Mansion and shot himself in the head. He was buried at Woodlawn Cemetery in Jefferson City.[42]

FEB 10

1841: Julia Soulard begins giving land to the City of St. Louis for use as a public market.

The oldest public market west of the Mississippi dates to the late 1700s, when Antoine Soulard married Julia Cerre. Cerre's father was given a massive plot of land by Spain, and he in turn gave it to his son-in-law. The plot included the area where the market was held. The Louisiana Purchase in 1803 put the ownership of the plot into question. Only after a decades-long legal dispute was Julia recognized as the owner of the land, her husband having died in the meantime. However, in 1841 Julia donated two city blocks of the land to the city with the provision that it would be home to a farmers market, which it remains today as Soulard Market.[43]

FEB 11 — 1856: The US Supreme Court hears the case of Dred Scott.

Courtesy Library of Congress

The landmark case had multiple ties to Missouri. Dred Scott was the "property" of the Peter Blow family in St. Louis in 1830. The Blows later sold Scott to Dr. John Emerson, a military doctor at Jefferson Barracks. Dr. Emerson later moved with Scott to Illinois and then to Wisconsin, where slavery had been outlawed. In 1846, after Emerson's family moved back to St. Louis, Dred Scott sued for his freedom on the grounds that he had lived in "free territory." The case of *Dred Scott v. Sandford* was first heard at the Old Courthouse in St. Louis. Later, in 1857, the high court ruled that slaves were not citizens, the Missouri Compromise was void, and African Americans were not entitled to citizenship, moving the country further toward civil war.[44]

FEB 12 — 1971: Missourian J. C. Penney dies at the age of 91.

J. C. Penney

James Cash Penney was a Missouri business icon who changed the retail industry while also changing millions of lives around the world. He started life humbly in the small town of Hamilton, where the family was taught the "Golden Rule." After graduating from school, he took a job at the Golden Rule Stores in Colorado. He saved enough money to purchase the store and renamed it the J.C. Penney Company. That was the beginning of a retail empire that saw him eventually open a store in every state. When Penney died, his stores across the country closed in his honor. He was remembered as a man who always said that he "didn't want a chain of stores, but a chain of good men."[45]

13 1920: The Negro National League is formed in Kansas City.

A meeting at the Paseo YMCA led by Rube Foster set the stage for a new baseball league that changed the face of the game forever. There were previous leagues for Black athletes that never proved to be sustainable, but this new organization promised to be different. The new league established teams across the Midwest and South, including baseball hotspots like St. Louis and Pittsburgh, along with Kansas City. The Kansas City Monarchs and St. Louis Giants proved to be two of the most successful teams of the young league, winning more than half of the titles. In fact, the Monarchs played in the Colored World Series twice, winning it all in 1924.[46]

14 2010: Jamie McMurray wins the Daytona 500.

There have been a handful of NASCAR drivers hailing from Missouri, including the legendary Wallace family from Arnold, Carl Edwards from Columbia, Larry Phillips from Springfield, and Ken Schrader from Fenton, but only one has been victorious at Daytona. Jamie McMurray from Joplin won the 52nd running of "The Great American Race" after defeating Dale Earnhardt Jr. Later in 2010, Murray also won the Brickyard 400, making him one of only three drivers to ever win both races in the same season.[47]

Courtesy Mike Kalasnik, Wikimedia Commons

The Spinks brothers

FEB 15 1978: Leon Spinks defeats Muhammad Ali.

In the late 1970s, millions of Americans would gather in front of their televisions to watch boxing matches for the "must-see tv" of the era. And if Muhammad Ali was on the title card, you can bet even more were glued to their sets. So, when the St. Louis boxer Leon Spinks stepped into the ring against "the Greatest," Missouri history was being made. It was Spinks's eighth professional bout, and Ali took him lightly as Spinks won the Undisputed Heavyweight Championship title in a split decision. *Sports Illustrated* put Spinks on the cover to commemorate the historic event.[48]

FEB 16 1847: The State Lunatic Asylum is approved to open in Fulton.

Missouri legislators wanted to address the problems of housing and treating people with mental health issues, many of whom were dangers to themselves and others. Accordingly, they approved the new facility, which was also called State Hospital Number 1. A group of 67 patients arrived at the first "insane asylum" west of the Mississippi during the first few weeks after it opened in 1851. As times changed and our understanding of mental health improved, the treatment and terminology used in state mental health institutions has also evolved. The building is now known as the Fulton State Hospital.[49]

FEB 17 1857: Iron County is established.

A special act by the Missouri Legislature led to the formation of Iron County, carved out of parts of Dent, Madison, Reynolds, St. Francois, Washington, and Wayne Counties. The area was becoming increasingly valuable, thanks in large part to mining operations that were sprouting up around the area. The name of the county and the county seat of Ironton both originated from the iron ore being mined.[50]

FEB 18

1859: City of Pacific is incorporated after changing its name.

A confusing situation led to the name change of the town that was once called Franklin. Another town in central Missouri was also named Franklin, which caused confusion. There were issues with mail and train service, as both towns were right along the rails. City leaders in the town that is now along Interstate-44 eventually decided to re-name the town Pacific in 1852 in honor of the Pacific Railroad running through downtown. Meanwhile, the town in central Missouri kept the name of Franklin, not to be confused with New Franklin just up the hill.[51]

FEB 19

1980: First Mardi Gras celebration is held in Soulard.

St. Louis now has the second-largest Mardi Gras celebration in the country, trailing only New Orleans. But it started small, with only a handful of friends who came together to throw a party at a house on Russell Boulevard and then marched to McGurk's Irish Pub. The party hit the big time in 1995 when 75-degree temperatures brought an estimated 250,000 partiers to the small neighborhood. In 1999, the party got out of control, as dozens of people were arrested and police had to use mace to disperse the crowds. The massive event now stretches for days and includes the Mayor's Mardi Gras Ball, a pet parade, and other events, bringing in hundreds of thousands of revelers each year.[52]

FEB 2003 19

Democratic Congressman Dick Gephardt announces his bid for presidency in the 2004 election. The St. Louis native was an early favorite heading into the Iowa caucuses, but dropped out after a poor showing.

20 2004: Albert Pujols signs a $100 million, seven-year deal with the Cardinals.

Pujols established himself as a force of baseball nature after arriving at Fort Osage High School, where he was a two-time Missouri All-State athlete. He then shattered records during his rookie year for St. Louis and continued his All-Star performances in the years that followed. The Cardinals made him the highest-paid player in team history with the new deal in 2004 as he proved his value for 11 seasons, winning MVP awards in 2005, 2008, and 2011. But he shocked fans after the 2011 World Series title, when he left St. Louis for a 10-year, $254-million deal with the Los Angeles Angels.[53]

21 1891: William T. Sherman is buried in the largest funeral procession in St. Louis history.

The body of the former Commanding General of the US Army was brought back to St. Louis to be buried in Calvary Cemetery after his death in New York. Sherman first moved to St. Louis first in 1850 with his new wife, but he moved during the war. After his service, Sherman moved back to St. Louis until President Ulysses S. Grant appointed him the general commander of the US Army. It was back at his house on North Garrison Avenue where Sherman sent the famous telegram after Republicans asked him to be their presidential nominee in 1884, stating, "I will not accept if nominated and will not serve if elected."[54]

FEB 22 — 1853: Washington University is founded as Eliot Seminary.

One of the most prestigious universities in America was founded after a local merchant and his pastor, William Greenleaf Eliot, became concerned about a lack of institutions for higher education in the area. The college was first organized under the charter of Eliot, Seminary, but organizers later chose the name Washington Institute of St. Louis. That name was changed again to Washington University three years later. By 1900, the college had outgrown its downtown location and construction began at the Hilltop campus. The university annually ranks as one of the top universities in the country.[55]

FEB 23 — 1983: The EPA announces its intent to buy all of Times Beach and evacuate the town.

Times Beach began as a resort town near the Meramec River, thanks to a promotion by the *St. Louis Star-Times* in 1925. If you purchased a subscription, you could buy a piece of land. The quaint river community was shocked when it was discovered that contaminated oil had been sprayed on roads in 1972. The EPA concluded that dioxin covered nearly all the land and that residents had to leave. Government agencies spent nearly $40 million to buy out the 800 properties as remediation began. By 1985, Times Beach was disincorporated. The land was cleaned and was reopened as Route 66 State Park.[56]

Lindenwood College for Women

FEB 24 — 1853: Lindenwood is chartered as a women's college.

One of the fastest-growing universities in the country had a humble beginning as the second college west of the Mississippi River. The university in St. Charles was incorporated by a special act of the Missouri Legislature as the Lindenwood College for Women, making it the oldest women's college in the "West." The initial name was Linden Wood, named after the linden trees on the campus. The college saw spectacular growth starting in 1989, when Dennis Spellman became campus president, and is now ranked as one of the finest colleges in the Midwest. In 1997, the school officially changed its name to Lindenwood University.[57]

FEB 25 — 1976: First rides given on the Screamin' Eagle.

After months of anticipation, select guests were finally allowed to ride a record-breaking roller coaster at Six Flags in Eureka. This event took on national interest as the amusement park unveiled a ride that changed the future of roller coasters.

The Screamin' Eagle was billed as the tallest, longest, and fastest roller coaster in existence, traveling at 62 miles per hour. It opened to the public on April 10, just in time for nationwide 1976 bicentennial celebrations. It was designated as a "Coaster Landmark" by the American Coaster Enthusiast on June 21, 2016.[58]

FEB 26 — 2004: Missouri Supreme Court rules that concealed weapons are constitutional.

A 5-2 decision by the state's highest court upheld the right of Missourians to carry a concealed gun, although the ruling caused another problem. The issue came before the court after Governor Bob Holden vetoed the law. Lawmakers then overrode his veto. Then came lawsuits that put the law on hold until the courts took up the case. They ruled in favor of the law, but also stated that counties didn't have to issue permits because it put an undue burden on sheriffs, who would have to cover the cost of implementation. Lawmakers eventually went back into session to find a way to pay for the new law.[59]

FEB 27 — 1851: Lawmakers kickstart "Plank Road Mania" in Missouri.

The plank road fad was taking America by storm in the mid-1800s as states did their best to connect towns as quickly as possible, as transportation methods were outgrowing the infrastructure. Plank roads were created when builders cut down trees and made roads out of the fallen timber. The wooden roads would help buggies get through rough and muddy areas. Missouri lawmakers passed laws that funded numerous road-building companies as they began additional projects across the state. In fact, the biggest, longest, and most planked road in America, the Missouri Plank Road, stretched over 42 miles, running from Sainte Genevieve through Farmington to Iron Mountain.[60]

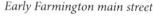

Early Farmington main street

FEB 28 — 1983: M*A*S*H finale ends with Missouri storylines.

One of the biggest TV events in history was seen by an estimated 120 million people, as the final episode of *M*A*S*H* aired on CBS. The television series was based on an award-winning movie directed by Kansas City's Robert Altman, and ran for 11 seasons. Missouri viewers especially loved the local storylines, including references to President Truman, and lead character Colonel Sherman Potter reminiscing about his home in Hannibal.[61]

Courtesy CBS Television, public domain, via Wikimedia Commons

FEB 29 — 1916: St. Louis voters approve racial segregation.

An overwhelming majority of city voters approved a racial zoning ordinance that legally mandated segregated living across the city. In the decade leading up to the vote, a large influx of African Americans had come to St. Louis from Southern states. The St. Louis Real Estate Exchange began an organized campaign, warning residents of declining property values if African Americans were allowed to move into certain neighborhoods, calling it a "Negro Invasion." In that 1916 vote, 74.5% of voters approved the measure that prohibited members of any race from moving into an area where 75% of residents were of another race. The US Supreme Court eventually outlawed the ordinance, but municipalities then put in place covenants (also later ruled unconstitutional) to keep homeowners from selling to Blacks.[62]

MARCH

MAR
01
1912: The first parachute jump from an airplane takes place in St. Louis.

US Army Captain Albert Berry made history when he got into an airplane, took off from Kinloch Field, and then jumped out over Jefferson Barracks Army Base. The Benoist biplane, piloted by Tony Jannus, was an open-air type of plane; Berry had to climb out of his and climb onto a trapeze-type bar, put on his parachute, then let go. The jump was only from 1,500 feet, but it took an estimated 500 feet for the chute to fill with air.[63]

MAR
02
1944: The Kansas City school board agrees to hire married women to teach.

In the years around World War II, women were being allowed new opportunities in the workforce, due to a severe shortage of workers. The Kansas City school district did not have enough teachers to fill classes, so they realized they had to open their ranks. Many women were already teaching, but districts across the state had barred married women from the jobs, so they could focus on duties at home. Times certainly have changed. As of 2019, more than 80% of all teachers nationwide were women.[64]

MAR 03   1911: The original Blonde Bombshell is born in Kansas City.

Jean Harlow was famous for movies, pinup posters, and her ability to make front-page news in Hollywood magazines. "The Platinum Blonde," as she was called from a 1931 movie of the same name, was the ultimate sex symbol and tabloid darling. She was also the precursor to today's troubled young stars, with money to burn and a life cut short. She became a celebrity when picked to star in the movie, *Hell's Angels.* A few years later, at the age of 26 while shooting *Saratoga,* she developed a sudden illness and died. The movie had to be finished with a body double and long-angle camera shots.[65]

MAR 04   1849: Senator David Rice Atchison becomes president for a day, or did he?

Long before Harry S. Truman, Missouri did have another man that can lay claim to being US president . . . for one day. Here is how it played out. Zachary Taylor had been elected president in 1848 to replace outgoing President James K. Polk. Polk's term ended at noon on Sunday, March 4, 1849. Taylor did not want to take the oath of office on a Sunday, so he postponed it until March 5. The law at the time read, "in case of the removal, death, resignation, or disability of both the President and Vice President of the United States, the President of the Senate Pro Tempore shall act as President." That is where Senator Atchison comes into play. Senator Atchison was serving as president of the Senate Pro Tempore at the time. So, for 24 hours, the man from Liberty was the acting president of the United States. The state of Missouri erected a monument in his honor in Plattsburg that reads, "David Rice Atchison. President of the US for one day. Lawyer, statesman and jurist."[66]

MAR 05 — 1946: Winston Churchill gives his "Iron Curtain" speech at Westminster College.

The Cold War was escalating in the years following World War II as the leaders of the free world realized they needed to take a strong stance against communism. So, the former British Prime Minister traveled to Fulton to condemn the policies of the Soviet Union. He was met by President Harry S. Truman, who just months earlier had made the decision to drop atomic bombs to bring the war to a close. Churchill used the phrase "Iron Curtain" in the speech to define the division between Western nations and Soviet powers. Russia said the speech escalated tension, while British and American allies saw it as a symbol of unity in decrying communist expansion.[67]

MAR 06 — 1981: Walter Cronkite's final broadcast.

The man who became "the most trusted man in America" was born in St. Joseph and grew up in Kansas City until he and his family moved to Texas. Cronkite returned to Missouri for his early years of broadcasting, at KCMO radio. Later in his career, as anchor of *The CBS Evening News*, he was the man viewers most turned to when President Kennedy was killed and when American astronauts landed on the moon. When he retired, millions tuned in for his final goodbye. A memorial was erected in his honor at Missouri Western State University in St. Joseph.[68]

Courtesy of the Library of Congress

MAR 07 — 2020: First COVID-19 case is reported in Missouri.

The Coronavirus Pandemic of 2020 impacted every aspect of life for all Americans and resulted in hundreds of thousands of deaths. When news of the virus first emerged, health care experts knew it was a matter of time before every state was impacted. In March, news broke that the virus had reached the Show-Me State. A 20-year-old student had tested positive after studying in Italy and traveling to St. Louis. It was later discovered that the virus had been in Missouri for at least a month prior, with a previous case being detected around February 2.[69]

MAR 2021 07

St. Louis natives Jayson Tatum and Bradley Beal team up in the NBA All-Star Game. It was a rare feat, as the two players from the same high school (Chaminade) played on the same All-Star team.

MAR 08 — 1836: The Missouri State Penitentiary gets its first prisoner.

Wilson Edison made history as the first inmate to be checked into the new prison in Jefferson City. He had the place to himself for a week, until inmate number two showed up. But this was not a place you wanted to stay for long. The State Pen eventually became known as "The bloodiest 47 acres in America" in light of its long history of murders, suspicious deaths, and executions. At one point, the overcrowded facility held more than 2,000 inmates, even holding men and women at times on Death Row. It was decommissioned in 2004 and is now a tourist site that hosts historical and paranormal tours.[70]

09 1872: Birthday of "The Missouri Giantess."

Ella Ewing was the world's tallest woman of her time. The 8'4" woman grew up in the small village of Gorin in northeast Missouri but traveled the country thanks to her fame. She was average size until the age of nine, when her growth spurt began. At first her family tried to keep her sheltered to protect her. Then her father realized that the only way she could get a job was to capitalize on her unique characteristic. She toured with the Barnum and Bailey Circus, where the

Ella Ewing

"lady giant" found a new family who accepted her as she was. She lived a short life of 40 years and was buried close to her childhood home.[71]

10 1963: Missouri's Supreme Court ends deliberations on Blue Laws, which prohibit shopping on Sunday.

According to the 137-year-old law, the only items that stores were able to sell were "articles of immediate necessity." The Supreme Court released its ruling the following day, March 11, stating that the laws were extremely vague and impossible to enforce. Almost as soon as the court ruled, some lawmakers immediately attempted to push through a "Sunday closing law." But residents overwhelmingly liked the idea of being able to purchase things on Sunday, and the contentious battles faded away. However, it took until 1975 before 5% beer could be sold on Sunday, with the abolition of the 1934 Liquor Control Law.[72]

11

1987: The Admiral riverboat opens again on the Mississippi River.

One of the most recognizable attractions along the St. Louis riverfront was back in business after being dormant for several years. The ship first arrived in St. Louis in 1940 and did daily sightseeing and dance cruises. The ship stopped cruising in the late 1970s, when the Coast Guard found structural weakness. The Six Flags corporation was a driving force behind the reopening in 1987, but the ship's second life was brief. The old boat opened one more time as the President Casino in 1994 and lasted until 2010, when it closed for good.[73]

12

1958: The greatest bowler of all time and his teammates smash a record.

St. Louis native Don Carter was a 10-time All-American and became known as "Mr. Bowling" over the course of his career. In fact, he became the first athlete of any kind to sign an endorsement deal for $1,000,000. In 1956, he moved back to St. Louis to join the Budweiser bowling team when he and legends Dick Weber, Ray Bluth, Tom Hennessey, and Pat Patterson set the American Bowling Congress' all-time scoring record at Floriss Lanes in St. Louis. All of them ended up in the Bowling Hall of Fame, and Carter was named the Greatest Bowler of All Time by *Bowling Magazine* in 1970.[74]

MAR 13

1942: Opening day at the home of Throwed Rolls.

Lambert's Café opened in Sikeston as a small cafe in southeast Missouri but expanded over the years to be more than just a restaurant. It is now a destination! Earl and Agnes Lambert opened the restaurant in on South Main Street with only eight tables and nine stools at the counter and a seating capacity of only 41. The Throwed Rolls phenomena began in 1976 when the owner's son was handing out rolls, but diners complained that they were not getting the rolls quickly enough. So, Norm Lambert began throwing rolls to serve customers more quickly, and the legend was born.

MAR 1964 13

The Beatles made their first concert appearance in St. Louis. They appeared in Kansas City on September 17.

MAR 14

1835: Missouri passes a bill requiring a "freedom license" for Blacks.

Legislators passed a bill which read, "all free persons of color had to apply for a freedom license." That law meant that not only did African Americans have to apply for freedom, but they also had to prove that they met the requirements required to be free, which was nearly impossible. The law was passed primarily because Missouri slave owners were concerned about free Blacks moving into Missouri and influencing existing slaves to rebel against their owners. A later law passed in 1847 was even more restrictive, prohibiting free Blacks from entering the state while also outlawing the education of Blacks already in the state.[75]

MAR 15

1931: Celebrations are held for the final section of Route 66 to be paved in Missouri.

It was a big party in downtown Rolla, as an estimated 8,000 people turned out to commemorate the completion of Route 66 across Missouri. The road dated back to 1922 as Route 14, but it was more of a dirt trail in some areas. The route was designated as a part of the National Highway System in 1926 and renamed US 60. The number changed again during a meeting at the Woodruff Building in Springfield, when it was renamed Route 66. The final section to be paved was between Rolla and Lebanon near the town of Arlington. In 1989, the Route 66 Association of Missouri formed to "preserve, promote, and develop" the highway that impacted America as much as any highway in history. Missouri was also the first state to put up a historic marker on Route 66 at Kearney Street and Glenstone Avenue in Springfield to forever commemorate the Main Street of America.[76]

MAR 16

1964: Walt Disney meets with St. Louis officials to discuss plans for the Riverfront Square theme park.

The headline in the *St. Louis Post-Dispatch* that morning read, "Disney reveals ideas of large amusement unit on riverfront." Walt had long wanted to build an entertainment complex in his home state. But his plans were met with resistance by locals, particularly August "Gussie" Busch Jr., who insisted that if a theme park were to be built at the site, Disney would have to sell beer. Disney became exceedingly frustrated with the opposition he was getting for his novel idea. But what really killed the deal was what was happening in central Florida. At the time, Disney was snapping up pieces of land near the small town of Orlando. He eventually realized that the Florida market offered a better opportunity, and a better climate, so he abandoned the plan in St. Louis and focused his efforts on the Sunshine State.[77]

38

MAR 17 | 1978: Kansas City's St. Patrick's Day Parade hits the big time.

Although the St. Patrick's Day Parade in downtown Kansas City is an annual tradition, it almost became just a memory. The event started in 1873 but declined significantly into the 1970s, when it was being called "the world's shortest and worst parade." Local Irish leaders had enough of the mediocrity and decided to resurrect the KC tradition in a major way. By 1981 it had gotten so popular that organizers had to move the event downtown, where an estimated 35,000 people turned out, making it the third-largest St. Patrick's Day parade in the country.

MAR 1992 17

Columbia native Sam Walton is presented with the Medal of Freedom from President George H.W. Bush. The Hickman High School and Mizzou alum founded Walmart in 1962 and had become the richest man in America by 1985.

MAR 18 | 1948: Saint Louis University wins the national basketball championship.

In the years before the NCAA Tournament and March Madness, college basketball's champion was crowned at the National Invitational Tournament (NIT). The NIT was held at Madison Square Garden and pitted New York University against the upstart team from Missouri, known as the Billikens. Led by coach Ed Hickey and star Ed Macauley, SLU defeated NYU 65-52 to win the title and finish the season 24-3. Making this an even better homegrown story, nearly all the Billiken players were from high schools in the St. Louis area, including five who had graduated from Saint Louis University High School.[78]

MAR 19 — 1875: Missouri Representative Isaac Parker becomes Judge Parker, later known as the "Hanging Judge."

Parker grew up in a politically connected family in Ohio before moving to St. Joseph as an adult to work as a lawyer. A decade after arriving in western Missouri, he won the Seventh District Congressional seat, which he held for four years. At that time President Ulysses S. Grant appointed him to the US District Court in Arkansas, where he became known as the "Hanging Judge." His court became known as "The Court of the Damned" due to the 160 death sentences he handed down.[79]

MAR 20 — 1920: Another Lemp family member commits suicide.

The Lemp Mansion in south St. Louis was once a place of wonder, as the wealthy family called the magnificent structure its home. But that home is now considered one of the most haunted places in America. The first tragedy was the 1901 death of Frederick Lemp at age 28 due to heart failure. He was the heir apparent to the Lemp Brewery and seemingly in good health. Three years later, on February 13, 1904, William Lemp Sr. shot himself. On March 20, 1920, Elsa Lemp Wright, to one of Frederick's sisters, shot herself at her own home. William Jr. shot himself on December 29, 1922, in the same room where his father killed himself. William III died elsewhere of a heart attack at 42. Brother Charles became the fourth member of the family to commit suicide, hanging himself on May 10, 1949. Most of the family members are now buried together at Bellefontaine Cemetery.[80]

MAR 1811 20

Birthday of "The Missouri Artist," George Caleb Bingham.

MAR 21 — 2006: Twitter is launched by Jack Dorsey.

Social media took a big step forward as St. Louis native Jack Dorsey sent out the very first tweet on the new platform called Twitter. Under the name @Jack, he tweeted out "just setting up my twttr." Thanks to Twitter and Dorsey's other business ventures, including Square, he became a billionaire before age 30. Twitter now has an estimated 145 million daily users, making it one of the most influential news distribution systems in the world.[81]

MAR 22 — 1913: Official state flag is finally adopted in Missouri.

Marie Watkins Oliver has become known as "Missouri's Betsy Ross" for designing our state flag. Oliver hailed from an influential family in Ray County, married a soon-to-be senator, and moved to Cape Girardeau. While he was practicing law, she was put in charge of the flag design in 1908. She took painstaking effort to incorporate everything Missouri stood for into the flag. Governor Elliot Major signed legislation recognizing the flag into law, and the original flag is now on display at the Secretary of State's office.[82]

MAR 23 1922: The first radio station west of the Mississippi gets a broadcast license.

WEW began its storied history on the campus of Saint Louis University and is recognized as the second-oldest radio station in America. WEW actually began operating about a decade earlier, broadcasting weather reports in Morse Code in 1912. When the station began playing music, Jesuit Brother George Rueppel, was one of the visionaries of the medium and began talking in between records, arguably making him the first radio DJ in history as well.[83]

MAR 24 2001: Southwest Missouri State University women upset #1 Duke University.

It was one of the biggest victories in the history of Missouri sports, as the Lady Bears defeated the Blue Devils to continue their run to the Final Four. In 2001, Jackie Stiles established Southwest Missouri State (now Missouri State University) basketball as one of the best women's programs in the country. She set the All-Time NCAA Division 1 scoring record while leading the team to a 29-6 record. The Women's Final Four was played at the Kiel Center in St. Louis, so it was a chance for Stiles to be on the national stage in front of the home-state fans. But in the National Semifinal, Purdue defeated the Lady Bears 81-64, bringing the season and Stiles's storied collegiate career to an end.[84]

MAR 2005 24

The Office debuts on NBC with Missourians in starring roles. Jenna Fischer, a Nerinx Hall and Truman State University graduate, played Pam Beesly while Phyllis Smith, a graduate of Cleveland High, played Phyllis Vance. Ellie Kemper of John Burroughs also worked on the show's production team.

MAR 25 1934: Springfield golfer Horton Smith wins the first-ever Masters.

Missouri native Horton Smith claimed the honors at the inaugural Augusta National Invitational, which later became known as The Masters. The 25-year-old golfer was one of the favorites to win at the Augusta National Golf Club, and he pulled through with a one-stroke victory in the four-day tournament. He won the event again two years later, also making him the first two-time winner of the Masters Tournament.[85]

MAR 26 1911: Tennessee Williams is born.

Tennessee Williams grew up in St. Louis, where he attended Soldan and University City High Schools before setting off for the University of Missouri–Columbia to further his education. It was at Mizzou that his real interest in writing began, but he had to return to St. Louis to find work to continue to pursue his dream. *The Glass Menagerie* was completed in 1944 and became his first real hit. He followed that with *The Night of the Iguana*, *A Streetcar Named Desire*, and *Cat on a Hot Tin Roof*. Those plays won him major awards, including the Pulitzer Prize and the New York Drama Critics' Circle Award. Tennessee's life came to an unceremonious end when he died from choking on a bottle cap at the age of 71 at his home in New York City. He was buried in St. Louis, even though he had asked to be buried at sea.[86]

MAR 1987 26

President Ronald Reagan arrives in Columbia via Air Force One. Reagan spoke to the National Governors Association at Hickman High School.

MAR 27

2017: For the fifth straight year, Webster University's Chess Team wins the National Championship.

Colleges in Missouri have had some amazing runs when it comes to national championships, from Saint Louis University's 10 soccer titles to Northwest Missouri State's six football titles. But only Webster University has won the President's Cup five consecutive times. The Gorloks eventually won seven straight titles, tying the collegiate record. St. Louis has become a world center of chess over the past two decades, thanks to the opening of the World Chess Club Hall of Fame in the Central West End neighborhood.[87]

MAR 28

1850: Kansas City is incorporated as a city.

The largest city in the state of Missouri had humble beginnings but grew into a major metro area at the confluence of the Missouri and Kansas rivers. Its key location had a vital impact on westward migration during American's early years, while also helping the city grow into a major transportation hub. The city has had three distinct "foundings" and three different names over its history. From Westport in 1830 to the Town of Kansas in later years, and eventually Kansas City in 1850, the city now has a population near 500,000 and is the 23rd largest city in the country.[88]

Courtesy of Missouri State Archives

MAR 29 **1995: Josephine Baker is inducted into the Hall of Famous Missourians.**

Baker was an international star and human rights activist known for her sultry vocals and distinct improvisational dance style as she discovered her ticket out of poverty through song and dance. Because of her strong views against racial discrimination, Baker left America for France to launch an entertainment career. She was instrumental in prompting nightclubs and theaters to integrate their audiences by refusing to perform unless nondiscriminatory seating practices were followed. One of the highlights of Baker's life was taking part in the 1963 Freedom March in Washington, D.C., and delivering a speech just before Dr. Martin Luther King Jr. at the Lincoln Memorial.[89]

MAR 2014 29

University of Central Missouri in Warrensburg wins the Division II Men's Basketball National Championship. The women's team won the National Title in 2018.

MAR 30 **1984: The official worldwide release of *Romancing the Stone*.**

Springfield native Kathleen Turner hits the big screen, starring alongside Michael Douglas in Romancing the Stone. The breakout hit propelled the Southwest Missouri State alum to A-list status after she won the Golden Globe award for best actress in a comedy.

Emerson Zooline Railroad, Courtesy Saint Louis Zoo

MAR 31 — 2017: The Saint Louis Zoo is named the best zoo in the nation.

Missourians have always been proud of the Saint Louis Zoo, and the world took notice when *USA Today* announced that the landmark had been named the best zoo by voters. To be voted on, the zoo first had to be handpicked by a panel of zoo and travel experts to make a list of 20 finalists. Making the award more impressive is that many of the other zoological parks on the list charge significant entrance fees, while the Saint Louis Zoo remains free. In 2018, the zoo won the prestigious honor for a second year in a row.[90]

APRIL

APR 01 **1912: The City of Branson is incorporated.**
Branson had been a long-established village along the banks of the White River since the late 1800s. The town saw rapid growth thanks to tourist attractions like Marble Cave and Lake Taneycomo in the early years, then Silver Dollar City, Highway 76 attractions, and Table Rock Lake in the years that followed. The city had a population of only 2,550 by 1980, but was seeing millions of tourists packing the small roads that meandered through the Ozark Mountain town. As more tourists, money, and attention came to

Branson, the city underwent a massive infrastructure campaign to get ready for future growth. By 2010, Branson boasted a population of 10,520 and hosted more than seven million visitors annually.[91]

APR 02 **1935: Kansas City jazz great Bennie Moten dies during a tonsillectomy.**
The "Kansas City Sound" was taking the nation by storm in the 1920s and '30s as the city was instrumental in transitioning from the orchestral era to a more improvisational style, with Moten as a key figure. He never got to see his music reach the masses, however, due to a botched surgery at the age of 40. He was undergoing a tonsillectomy at Wheatley-Provident Hospital in Kansas City when he died during the procedure. One of his bandmates, Count Basie, took the reins of the movement and made Kansas City a hub for jazz and blues, while paving the way for a new style of music known as Bebop.[92]

APR 03
1882: Jesse James is killed in St. Joseph.

Jesse James and his family were on the run when they rented a house in St. Joseph to hide. Robert Ford was one of the only people James trusted. But James didn't know that Ford had been communicating with Missouri Governor Thomas Crittenden to help capture him. During a visit, Ford shot Jesse from behind while James was adjusting a picture on the wall. Ford then alerted the governor about what he had done and was ready to collect the reward. Ford was then charged with murder, sentenced to hanging, then pardoned by the Missouri governor, all in a single day.[93]

APR 04
1887: Springfield and North Springfield merge to become one city.

There is a reason why Division Street has its name. North Springfield and the city of Springfield were two separate municipalities for about 15 years before voters agreed to merge. Division Street had long been the dividing line. On the night the merger was approved, residents gathered on the Springfield square to shoot off fireworks and celebrate. Although Division Street remains, there was an effort to rename it Union Street to help the new city function as a single entity.[94]

APR 2006 04

A third version of Busch Stadium opens in St. Louis. The first game showcased the St. Louis Cardinals' minor league affiliates, the Memphis Redbirds and the Springfield Cardinals, while the St. Louis Cardinals took the field a week later. The very first year in their new stadium, the Cardinals won the World Series.

APR 05

1921: The citizens of St. James elect the first female mayor in the state.

Two years after women in Missouri were finally allowed to vote, the first female mayor in Missouri history was elected in St. James. Mayme Ousley grew up in nearby Edgar Springs but moved to St. James after her husband graduated from dental school and set up his practice. Women were highly motivated to vote following the passage of the 19th Amendment, and now they had a woman they could vote for. She won the election by only eight votes but made history in the process.[95]

APR 06

2020: Missouri's governor issues a "Shelter in Place" order to slow the spread of the coronavirus.

The order specified that all people residing in the state of Missouri avoid leaving their homes unless necessary. That COVID-19 order also drew anger from residents, as it restricted gatherings across the state to 10 or fewer people, closed schools for the rest of the semester, capped occupancy of most businesses at 25% of normal operating capacity, and required social distancing. The order would stay in place until April 24. One thing Governor Mike Parson's order did not do, which public health officials had been requesting, was issue a statewide mask mandate.[96]

APR 07 | 1939: Democratic political boss Tom Pendergast is indicted on income tax charges.

Pendergast was arguably the most powerful man in Missouri, and possibly one of the most influential in the nation, in the two decades leading up to his fall. During his reign as leader of the "Pendergast Political Machine," he controlled practically everything that happened in business and politics in the Kansas City area and, by extension, in Jefferson City as well. His empire came crumbling down, thanks in large part to one of the politicians he helped climb the ranks. Governor Lloyd Stark urged federal authorities to investigate

Tom Penderhast

Pendergast's dealings, leading to federal tax evasion charges, prison time, and eventually, the decline of his political machine.[97]

APR 1933 07

Beer containing 3.2% alcohol is legal at midnight.

Governor Lloyd Stark

1969: The Kansas City Royals play their first game ever.

Kansas City had been left without a team for two years after the Athletics bolted for Oakland in 1967, so it was a time of spring renewal, as the city had a team to root for again. The Royals took their name from the world-famous American Royal livestock show and barbecue competition that is held annually in town, along with it being the name of two Negro League teams. The team played in the old Municipal Stadium until Royals Stadium was ready in 1973. The name was changed to Kauffman Stadium in 1993 in honor of founder Ewing Kauffman.[98]

1917: The State Park Fund is created to develop Missouri state parks.

One year after the National Park System was established in 1916, the state of Missouri put a funding mechanism in place to preserve designated areas of land and transform them into public spaces. The first piece of property bought was the J. Huston Tavern in Arrow Rock six years later. The first piece of land established as a state park was Big Spring State Park near Van Buren. There are now 91 state parks along with the Katy Trail, which is the longest "rails to trails" project in United States history.[99]

J. Huston Tavern

APR 10 — 1961: McDonald County secedes from Missouri.

McDonald County became known as McDonald Territory for several months by the locals after several perceived "slights" by the state of Missouri. First, Highway 71 was rerouted around Noel, which impacted local businesses. Then, the highway department released new maps with several McDonald County towns left off, hurting local tourism. This was either an honest mistake or a major insult, so county leaders declared independence from the state. They proposed being annexed into Arkansas or Oklahoma or even becoming the 51st state. The publicity was good, and the two sides eventually reconciled, but only after territorial stamps and visas had already been printed.[100]

APR 11 — 1842: Charles Dickens visits Missouri and is not impressed.

The English author came to America in 1842 prior to his 30th birthday to see the young country for himself. Even though he was at the height of his popularity and the audiences to see him were large, he was often in a foul mood, likely because he liked solitude. When he arrived in St. Louis, he was impressed by the architecture but didn't think the city would ever measure up to other places he had seen, like Cincinnati. He also wrote that he enjoyed the open spaces outside of the city and the visits with people like William Greenleaf Eliot. Even though he did offer up some negative views about the city, including slavery, his visit wasn't as negative as it is often portrayed.[101]

Truman house in Independence

APR 12 1945: Harry S. Truman becomes President Truman.

The "plain-speaking man from Missouri" became the most powerful man in the world when he assumed the title of president after the sudden death of Franklin Delano Roosevelt. Truman spent his childhood living in several Missouri towns, including Lamar, where he was born, and Grandview, where he spent his early years on the family farm. His family eventually moved to Independence so Harry could attend school there.

Truman bounced around careers ranging from railroad timekeeper to bank clerk to farmer in Grandview, where he lived for eight years before his father died. He also served in the National Guard, where his military career swung into high gear as the United States entered World War I. After the war he returned to Independence, married Bess Wallace, and opened a clothing store in Kansas City, which eventually failed, leading Truman to a career in politics.

Truman was elected to the US Senate in 1935 and served until he became vice president in 1945. Then, only 82 days into the term, FDR died, leaving Truman as the 33rd president in the midst of World War II. Truman was elected by voters in 1948 and served until 1953.

His tenure as president will be forever marked by his decision to use the atomic bombs on Japan, but he will also be remembered for the development of the Cold War policy of containment. He often said that when his time in the Oval Office was done, he was going to return to Missouri to become "Mr. Citizen," which is exactly what he did.[102]

APR 2004 12
Miss Missouri, Shandi Finnessey, wins Miss USA.

1928: The West Plains dance hall explosion kills 39.

The tragedy in the southern Missouri town impacted nearly everyone in the community. The blast happened at 11:05 p.m., as the dance floor was crowded with couples while the band was playing one final song. The explosion sent bodies flying and was felt more than three miles away. By the time everyone was accounted for, 39 people were confirmed dead. There are several theories about what caused the blast, but most point to gasses under the building that somehow ignited. The local newspaper reported as many as 7,000 people attended the memorial service.[103]

APR 1996 13

Major League Soccer comes to Missouri when the Kansas City Wiz entered the league as a charter team. The team is now known as Sporting KC.

1906: A mob lynches three Black men on the Springfield square.

Springfield history was forever changed as a mob abducted three Black men and lynched them on the public square. False accusations of rape and robbery were made against Horace Duncan and Fred Coker, and they were arrested with no evidence. Townsfolk stormed the jail and abducted the two innocent men and dragged them to the square. Thousands watched as the men were hanged and their bodies set on fire. Following the hanging, the crowd went back to the jail and abducted another man, Will Allen, who was also marched to the square and hanged. Many Blacks living in Springfield fled the city, significantly decreasing the Black population for years to come.[104]

APR 1922 14

Jack Taylor is born in St. Louis. He went on to found Enterprise Rent-A-Car in 1957, becoming one of America's richest men in the process.

APR 15 — 1889: Thomas Hart Benton is born in Neosho.

One of Missouri's early icons was raised in southwest Missouri before he became one of the most famous artists in America in the 1900s. He helped develop the regionalist movement, which exposed lives of average Americans in the Midwest to a broader audience. He came from one of Missouri's most influential families and is often confused with his great uncle and namesake, Senator Thomas Hart Benton.[105]

APR 16 — 1857: One of the nation's "smartest and most interesting people" is born on a farm in Fayette.

Henry Smith Pritchett had the blessing of being born to a brilliant professor and college president, Carr Waller Pritchett, who was the director of the Morrison Observatory. Henry was educated at Pritchett College (named after his family) in Glasgow, Missouri, then later at the US Naval Observatory as an astronomer. Later in life, he became the president of Massachusetts Institute of Technology (MIT) for a time. But his most enduring work was as the first president of the Carnegie Foundation for the Advancement of Teaching, where he was handpicked by Andrew Carnegie for the role.[106]

Left: *Pritchett College*
Below: *Carr Waller Pritchett*

APR 17 — 1892: Fountain Day begins in Kansas City.

Kansas City is known for its water features, ranking behind only Rome in the number of fountains. The earliest ones in Kansas City were built out of necessity for horses and dogs to drink from and cool off. The fountains built in the early 1900s were more ornate and unique to their neighborhoods. Many of them fell into disrepair over the years until a local couple toured Italy, fell in love with the structures, and decided to bring the KC fountains back to life. There are now more than 200 across the city, with most opening on the annual Fountain Day.[107]

APR 1945 17

Harry Caray calls his first game as the official voice of the St. Louis Cardinals. In 1954, he was paired with Jack Buck.

APR 18 — 2008: The Green Switch Celebration is held in Rock Port.

The small town on the windswept plains of northwest Missouri became the first community in America to generate 100% of its electricity from wind power. The four turbines generate twice as much power as the town of 1,300 residents in Atchison County requires.

APR 2017 18

Tiger Woods appears with Bass Pro Shops founder Johnny Morris to unveil a new golf course in Branson, "Payne's Valley."

APR 19

1983: The St. Louis Blues are sold by Ralston Purina to a group in Saskatchewan for $12 million.

The deal had been in the works for months after the CEO of Ralston Purina decided his company needed to focus on pet food products, not hockey. Fans were shocked when the deal was announced with the small town of Saskatoon, which had fewer than 200,000 residents. The NHL was also shocked and intervened to block the deal. Ralston filed an antitrust suit, while the NHL filed a countersuit for damages. A new buyer, Harry Ornest, became the only bidder for the team, and the Blues stayed in St. Louis.[108]

APR 20

1982: Thousands of bowling fans attend the groundbreaking for the International Bowling Hall of Fame.

St. Louis had been at the epicenter of bowling for decades, as some of the world's top bowlers had grown up on the lanes in Missouri or had moved here to perfect their craft. So, it only made sense that a hall of fame to celebrate their achievements be based in the city where they became famous. The museum drew tens of thousands of fans each year, but moved to Texas when the building was demolished to make way for Busch Stadium III.

APR 21

1955: The first polio vaccines arrive in Missouri.

Like nearly every state in the 1950s, Missouri was facing the viral scourge of polio that for decades had left its victims with crippling deformities, paralyzed, or even dead. Finally, in early 1955, the "miracle cure" discovered by Dr. Jonas Salk was being distributed to states. The first shipment of the vaccine arrived via Trans World Airlines at Wheeler Airport in Kansas City and via trains in downtown St. Louis. Salk refused a patent on the vaccine, so it could be distributed without restrictions, and he became one of the most famous scientists in the world for his discovery.[109]

Wilson's Creek National Battlefield dedication

APR 22 · 1960: Wilson's Creek National Battlefield is established.

The battle at Wilson's Creek was the first major battle in Missouri's long Civil War history. The battle took place on August 10, 1861, west of Springfield, as there was a serious effort underway for Missouri to secede from the Union. Southern-sympathizing soldiers first arrived on the land to come up with battle plan. Federal forces launched a surprise attack, and the battle went on for hours. More than 1,000 troops on each side were killed and lying across the rolling hills. President Dwight D. Eisenhower officially recognized the historical significance of the battle and preserved the land for later generations to study and honor.[110]

APR 23 · 1967: James Earl Ray escapes from the Missouri State Penitentiary.

Ray was doing 20 years for a robbery when he escaped in a bread truck. It wasn't even big news at the time until one year later, when Dr. Martin Luther King Jr. was killed in Memphis on April 4, 1968. Investigators found fingerprints on a rifle in a flophouse across the street from the Lorraine Motel. Those fingerprints were later matched to a set of prints housed in Jefferson City of a small-time thief who had escaped from the State Pen.[111]

APR 24 · 1990: The Hubble Space Telescope is launched into orbit.

The Space Shuttle Discovery launched into space one of the most powerful observatories ever created, and now a household name. But at the time, few people knew the Missouri connection. The Hubble Space Telescope was named after Edwin Hubble, known as the "Father of Modern Cosmology." Hubble grew up in Marshfield before becoming a world leader in astrophysics, where he came up with "Hubble's Law," which states that galaxies are moving away from earth, and that the further a galaxy is away from earth, the faster it is moving into space.[112]

APR 25 · 1969: Broadcaster Joe Buck is born.

Although there is no way Joe could remember the day of his birth, he certainly remembered his 17th birthday. Joe was attending a St. Louis Cardinals game in the broadcast booth with his father, broadcaster Jack Buck. Jack walked out of the booth and left young Joe there alone to do the play-by-play. Joe later became a star in his own right as the lead broadcaster for Fox, where he has called the Super Bowl and World Series several times. The family has made many "firsts" as broadcasters, including being the first father-son duo to win the Rozelle Award, putting both in the Pro Football Hall of Fame.

APR 26 — 1960: Ed Macauley becomes the youngest player ever inducted into the NBA Hall of Fame at age 32.

Macauley was a basketball legend in St. Louis, having helped the St. Louis Hawks become one of the most dominant teams of the 1950s. He also starred at Saint Louis University High, and then at Saint Louis University. He was named the national college basketball player of the year in 1949 and the MVP of the NBA's first All-Star Game in 1951. He made the All-Star team in seven of his 10 seasons as a pro.[113]

APR 27 — 1822: President Ulysses S. Grant is born.

Missouri has had only one "official" president it can claim as its own. But perhaps no other president spent more time in Missouri than Ulysses S. Grant. Grant was from Ohio but moved to Missouri in 1843, when the US Army sent him to Jefferson Barracks after he graduated from West Point. It was in St. Louis that Grant met his future wife, Julia Dent. Although the couple left for a few years, they found themselves back in Missouri during the Civil War when Colonel Grant was put in charge of troops in the area. His connection to Missouri is immortalized at Grant's Farm, named in his honor, and at the Ulysses S. Grant National Historic site in Grantwood Village.[114]

APR 28

2012: A hailstorm blasts through downtown St. Louis as Cardinals fans are celebrating.

The Cardinals had just wrapped up a game against the Milwaukee Brewers and were still celebrating near Busch Stadium. A severe storm developed quickly at around 4 p.m. and delivered some of its strongest blows to downtown. A beer tent at nearby Kilroy's Sports Bar was sent airborne by the wind as hail pounded fans running for cover. One man was killed, and approximately 100 others were injured. The storm ended up being one of the most damaging and costly hailstorms in American history, with approximately $42 billion in insured loses.[115]

APR 29

1927: The *Spirit of St. Louis* is completed, and Charles Lindbergh takes it for a test flight.

Although the flight happened in San Diego, there was significant attention paid to this flight in Missouri. This revolutionary plane that was destined to make the first transatlantic flight had been paid for mostly by families from St. Louis. Many of those sponsors were in California that morning to see Lucky Lindy test out the monoplane in a series of stunts. Days after completion, Lindbergh flew the plane to St. Louis for locals to see, and then it was off to New York a month later for the history-making flight.[116]

APR 1995 29

John Nonely of the Kansas City Royals becomes only the 70th player in MLB history to hit a home run in his very first time at bat.

APR 1904: World's Fair opens in St. Louis.

30

What is perhaps the biggest event in the city's history officially opened to the public with the eyes of the world on St. Louis. The city had been preparing to host the Louisiana Purchase Exposition for years, and everything came together in time for an estimated 20 million visitors to the fair grounds. It was truly a worldwide event, as more than 50 countries participated over the course of its seven-month run. By the time the event was over, the city of St. Louis was being hailed as a world-class city that had literally changed the world regarding architecture, food, entertainment, and culture.

APR 1926 30

A meeting is held in Springfield to resolve a dispute over the numbering of the new highway being built through the city. After a compromise, the historic telegram is sent to Washington, DC, with the new name: Route 66.

MAY

MAY 01 **1960: Silver Dollar City opens to the public.**

The theme park near Branson opened directly above Marvel Cave to an enthusiastic reception. The 1880s Ozark Mountain–themed park started relatively small, with only a handful of stores, a church, a log cabin, and a production based on the Hatfields and McCoys. The park got national attention in 2007 when ABC's *Good Morning America* named its Christmas festival one of the top five in the country. The park has grown into a world-class attraction, even being named "America's Best Theme Park" by *USA Today* in 2020.[117]

MAY 1958 01

The KATY train that ran across the state of Missouri made its final trips. The cars were packed with passengers who wanted to be the final riders on the rail line.

MAY 02 **1861: Governor Claiborne Jackson makes the final decision to have state militia assemble at Camp Jackson.**

The Missouri governor wanted the state to secede from the Union, so tensions were already high. Weeks prior, Jackson had told President Lincoln that he would not assemble troops from Missouri to fight against the South. Instead, he ordered Missouri Volunteer Militia troops to assemble near St. Louis, where he devised a plan to attack the US Arsenal and take the weapons stored there. The plan was foiled; the weapons were moved before the attack, and hundreds of Union troops were secretly sent in to surround the militia members, who were ultimately taken prisoner.[118]

PROCLAMATION

Head Quarters Western Department,
ST. LOUIS, MO. August 14, 1861.
I hereby declare and establish

Martial Law

In the City and County of St. Louis.

Major J. McKINSTRY, U. S. Army,
is appointed Provost Marshal. All orders
and regulations issued by him will be respected and obeyed.

J. C. FREMONT,
Major General Commanding

MAY 03 | 1948: The US Supreme Court rules in the case of *Shelley v Kraemer*.

The groundbreaking St. Louis legal case drew the attention of the country as a Black family sued after buying a home where they weren't allowed to live. The case dated back to 1911, when more than three dozen property owners entered into a restrictive covenant that blocked Blacks and Asians from buying property in that neighborhood. The Shelleys didn't know about the covenant until after they bought the home. Other homeowners sued to block them from taking possession of the property. The high court ultimately struck down most restrictive housing covenants as discriminatory and in violation of the Equal Protection Clause of the 14th Amendment.[119]

MAY 04 | 2003: Tornadoes rip through the Missouri, killing nearly two dozen.

This date brings back nightmares to many in southwest Missouri, as towns including Battlefield, Stockton, and Pierce City were devastated by tornadoes. In that area alone, 18 people died due to the storms. The system produced more severe storms than had been seen in any other week in US history, with May 4th being the worst day of that sequence. As the Springfield area was being hammered, tornadoes also broke out in North Kansas City and Gladstone, which were hit with F4 tornadoes, and Liberty, which endured an F2. The following day, Jackson was hit by an F3.[120]

MAY 05 — 1961: Alan Shepard becomes the first American in space.

The United States' first manned spaceflight captured the attention of the world as Alan Shepard blasted off onboard the Mercury-Redstone 3 space capsule. Missouri residents had a special reason to watch the liftoff of Project Mercury: the capsule itself had been manufactured at McDonnell Aircraft. An estimated 45 million Americans watched the Freedom 7 streak skyward for the 15-minute suborbital flight before Shepard splashed down in the North Atlantic Ocean, providing evidence that the human body could withstand high g-forces along with atmospheric re-entry.[121]

MAY 06 — 2016: Kansas City unveils new streetcar system.

What is old became new again as the KC streetcar system opened to the public. Voters approved the system in 2012, as the city was looking for ways to modernize its transit system and make its growing downtown area more accessible without the need for cars. The streetcars run between River Market and Union Station with downtown Kansas City in between, and they became a nearly instant success, with nearly 6,500 riders per day by 2019.[122]

MAY 07 — 2009: Mickey Carroll dies at the age of 89.

Although you may not remember the name, you will certainly remember the character he played. Carroll was raised in St. Louis, but according to his own words, he never really grew up. Carroll stood a little over three feet tall when he was cast to appear as the Munchkin town crier in *The Wizard of Oz*. After his Tinseltown success, he came back to Missouri, where he ran his family's business, the Standard Monument Company. In 2007, he was immortalized when he and the few surviving Munchkins received a star on the Hollywood Walk of Fame.[123]

MAY 08 | 1898: The St. Louis Motor Carriage Company is founded.

George Preston Dorris and John French founded the first automobile manufacturing company in Missouri on North Vandeventer Avenue. The company only lasted eight years, but paved the way for St. Louis to become an early hub for automobile manufacturing. One of its first models was the iconic "Runabout," which seated four passengers. The revolutionary "St. Louis" came along a few years after. French moved the company to Peoria, Illinois, in 1906, while Dorris expanded his own operations by starting the Dorris Motor Car Company the same year.[124]

MAY 09 | 1840: Mastodon bones are discovered in Missouri.

Although the exact date of discovery is unknown, it was around this day that a farmer near current-day Imperial found large fossils that he wanted inspected. It was also around this era that the famous "fossil showman" Albert Koch was making up outlandish exhibits showcasing unusual things that he found around the world,

often taking artistic and scientific liberties. Koch quickly secured the rights to excavate the bones and began to assemble the skeletal system of an animal that, in fact, never did exist. The bones were those of several mastodons, but Koch reconfigured them into one gigantic beast. He even added a few missing "pieces" to create what he called the Missouri Leviathan. He showcased the unique specimen across North America and eventually in Europe to great fanfare. Koch sold the specimen for a sizable fee to the British Natural History Museum, where they eventually took the beast apart and made it more anatomically accurate.[125]

MAY 10 | 1957: African American entrepreneur Annie Pope Malone dies.

Annie Malone grew her small business into a household name in the early 1900s, making her one of the wealthiest women in St. Louis and one of the first Black millionaires in the country. In 1902, at the age of 32, she opened a hair care business specializing in hair products designed specifically for African Americans. Even though she started out by selling door to door, her Poro business exploded as the World's Fair came to town. Malone also opened beauty schools in more

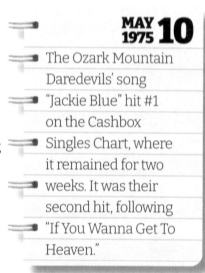

MAY 1975 10

The Ozark Mountain Daredevils' song "Jackie Blue" hit #1 on the Cashbox Singles Chart, where it remained for two weeks. It was their second hit, following "If You Wanna Get To Heaven."

than a dozen cities. She donated large sums of money to the St. Louis Colored Orphans Home, which eventually became the Annie Malone Children's Home.[126]

MAY 11 | 2011: The "Population Center of the United States" is moved to Plato.

The center of the United States' population is determined in a rather unique way. According to the Census Bureau, the center of population is "the place where an imaginary, flat, weightless and rigid map of the United States would balance perfectly if all 308,745,538 residents counted in the Census were of identical weight." The population center, of course, started along the East Coast when the country was founded and has steadily moved west. It moved into Missouri in 1980, when it was in Jefferson County. In 1990, it moved to Steelville; in 2000 it landed in Edgar Springs, south of Rolla; and the 2010 Census moved it to Plato. If the movement continues at its average pace, the population center is estimated to be somewhere between Hartville and Springfield, following the 2020 count.[127]

12 1925: Yogi Berra is born on The Hill.

Lawrence Berra was one of the most colorful and talented characters ever to play baseball. He grew up in the Italian neighborhood of St. Louis alongside childhood friend Joe Garagiola. He took on the nickname "Yogi" because his friends thought he resembled a Hindu holy man they had seen in a movie. Yogi hit a home run in his first Major League game and never looked back. He played in 14 World Series Championships with the Yankees and was inducted into the Baseball Hall of Fame in 1972 in recognition of his career as both a player and coach.[128]

13 1946: Bell Systems announces that car phones will make nationwide debut in Missouri.

Although most people mistakenly believe that cellular phones came out in the 1980s, they actually made their debut about 40 years earlier. The big announcement from the telephone company was big news for St. Louis, which was to be the first city to have this sort of communication service in a car. The early phones weighed around 80 pounds, with a massive price tag to boot. Following the debut of the service in Missouri on June 17, 1946, it was expanded to nearly 100 other cities across the country.[129]

14 1804: The Lewis and Clark Expedition sets out across Missouri.

William Clark and Meriwether Lewis led their 45-man crew out of St. Charles to explore the lands west of the Mississippi River. The United States had just acquired much of the land via the Louisiana Purchase, yet had little idea what the land contained. The team returned to St. Louis about two years later, on September 23, 1806. Lewis became the territorial governor, and Clark helped the region develop prior to its becoming a state.[130]

MAY 15 | 1850: Bellefontaine Cemetery, the final home of the rich and famous, is dedicated in St. Louis.

This cemetery was established to help alleviate overcrowding at other cemeteries as the city boomed. Planners picked a rural location where the dead could be laid to rest in a park-like setting. After a spot in the quiet countryside northwest of the city limits was chosen, designs were laid out with an elaborate chapel and peaceful setting. In time, the cemetery became the final resting place for a virtual "who's who" of St. Louis.[131]

MAY 16 | 1910: The high-profile Swope Murder Case concludes ... for a time.

One of the most shocking murder cases in Kansas City history went to trial after Dr. Bennett Clark Hyde was charged with killing local philanthropist Thomas Swope. Swope was a wealthy developer and the namesake for Swope Park. Dr. Hyde was his physician and was married to his niece. Prosecutors believed the doctor killed the local icon in order to secure a larger inheritance. The jury came back with a guilty verdict, shocking people around the country who had been following the case closely. The verdict was later overturned, making Dr. Hyde a free man, but the allegations followed him until he died in Lexington decades later.[132]

MAY 1998 16

Mark McGwire hits the longest home run in Busch Stadium II history, at 545 feet.

MAY 17

1956: Elvis performs at the Shrine Mosque, after briefly disappearing.

A rather bizarre situation unfolded in downtown Springfield when Elvis Presley came for a concert at the Shrine Mosque. After a quick sound check, the 21-year-old, up-and-coming star was nowhere to be found as showtime was getting closer. He was eventually found at the nearby Gillioz Theater, watching a Glenn Ford western movie. He had apparently needed to collect his thoughts, so he left the Shrine Mosque without telling anyone.[133]

MAY 18

1849: The Great St. Louis Riverfront Fire rages.

The fire had broken out the previous evening and was getting stronger as it jumped from building to building along the Mississippi riverfront. It took more than 11 hours before it was finally brought under control. 418 buildings were destroyed, as the face of the city was forever changed. Much of the area that was burned is where Laclede's Landing and the Gateway Arch now stand. The incident forced changes to building codes to make sure that an incident like this could never happen again.[134]

MAY 19

1907: 53,000 Kansas Citians turn out for the grand opening of Electric Park.

The theme park was the brainchild of the Heim family, who operated the massive Heim Brewing Company. The park opened near 46th and Paseo, with 100,000 lights illuminating attractions like a roller coaster, a carousel, a swimming pool, a skating rink, dance halls, arcades, and even an alligator farm. It remained a popular destination for years, with an estimated one million people visiting the park annually. Interestingly, Walt Disney and his sister regularly attended the park as kids, and a nine-year-old named Walter Cronkite witnessed the 1925 fire at the park that hastened its demise.[135]

20 1927: Charles Lindbergh departs for Paris in the *Spirit of St. Louis.*

Courtesy Missouri History Museum

Lindbergh took off early in the morning from Roosevelt Field on Long Island, New York, to make the first nonstop flight from America to France. "Lucky Lindy" likely never would have been able to make the flight, had it not been for influential backers in St. Louis who Lindbergh had befriended while flying mail routes between St. Louis and Chicago. The *Spirit of St. Louis* was not only the name of the plane, but also both a nod to the wealthy families that helped finance the expedition and a reference to his goal of making St. Louis the central hub of the aviation industry.[136]

21 1947: Jackie Robinson makes his debut in St. Louis at Sportsman's Park.

History was made at the stadium on Grand Boulevard as the league's first African American baseball player played for the first time in Missouri with the Brooklyn Dodgers. Robinson had broken the color barrier only a month prior, on April 15, and the racial animosity was evident in every city where the team played. At the time, St. Louis was the southernmost city in Major League Baseball, and there were reports that the team was going to boycott the game. The team played in front of the largest weekday crowd of the season, with an estimated "6,000 negroes" in attendance, according to press reports.[137]

MAY 2008 21
Blue Springs native David Cook wins season seven of *American Idol.*

MAY 22 2011: An EF5 tornado strikes Joplin, killing at least 158 people.

One of the strongest tornadoes ever recorded in Missouri struck Joplin, destroying virtually everything in its path. The EF5 tornado, with winds of over 200 mph, was up to three-quarters of a mile wide and stayed on the ground for 46 minutes as it carved a path through the middle of the city. The supercell twister cut a path eastward through the city, destroying 5,000 buildings and damaging another 2,500. By the time the skies cleared, it was one of the costliest tornadoes in US history, with damages estimated at $2.8 billion.[138]

MAY 23 1968: Wainwright Building is added to the National Register of Historic Places.

One of the first skyscrapers in America rose from the ground in 1891 to forever change the skyline of St. Louis. At the time the Wainwright Building was erected by Louis Wainwright, St. Louis was the fourth-largest city in America and growing rapidly, so it was no surprise that one of the first mammoth buildings was built in the city. At 10 stories tall it towered over the city, trailing only the tower of the Old Courthouse in height. The structure has been named by PBS as one of the "Ten Buildings that Changed America."[139]

MAY 1922 23

Laugh-O-Gram Films was incorporated in Kansas City by 20-year-old Walt Disney.

MAY 24

2017: Supermodel Karlie Kloss wins the Diane Von Furstenberg Inspiration Award.

Webster Groves native Karlie Kloss strutted across catwalks around the world to rise to the top of her industry at a young age. She became a top supermodel, making millions of dollars a year by gracing the covers of international *Vogue* magazines more than 40 times. The one-time Victoria's Secret runway model used her worldwide fame to branch into other ventures, including starting a series of computer classes called Kode with Klossy to get young girls interested in coding. She also partnered with other investors to buy *W Magazine* to put a larger footprint on her empire.[140]

Karlie Kloss, courtesy of Bethany Wong, Wikimedia Commons

MAY 25

1901: Glen Echo Country Club opens.

The first golf course west of the Mississippi opened in Normandy as a club for affluent St. Louisans to escape the pressures of city living. The private club in Normandy was founded by two prominent citizens, George McGrew and Albert Bond Lambert. At one point in its history, Glen Echo even had its own train stop so members could easily get there. The course was the site of the 1904 Olympic Golf Tournament and also hosted several LPGA Tour events.[141]

1973: Worlds of Fun amusement park opens.

26

Local icon Lamar Hunt was the driving force behind the theme park based off the novel, *Around the World in 80 Days*. Kansas City was booming, with a new airport, the Kemper Arena, and other major projects, so Hunt and his business partner, Jack Steadman, wanted to develop something unique for the city. In 1976, Worlds of Fun got the attention of the world with the first stand-up looping roller coaster in North America. The park expanded further in 1982 with the opening of Oceans of Fun, which was listed as the largest water-based theme park in the world.[142]

1911: Vincent Price is born in St. Louis.

27

One of America's best-known character actors was born into a wealthy and influential family, with little indication of the type of fame that was to come. Price's father was the president of the National Candy Company, and his grandfather was the inventor of Dr. Price's Baking Powder. That privileged upbringing allowed Vincent to pursue his passion in the arts, especially acting. The classically trained actor first rose to fame with *House of Wax* in 1954, which he followed with dozens of other starring roles. But younger people may remember him best as the creepy voice in Michael Jackson's song, "Thriller." [143]

MAY
28 1819: The first steamboat on the Missouri River arrives at Franklin.

It may not seem that monumental today, but a riverboat traveling upstream to the town of Franklin was a big deal as the state was being established. In the early 1800s, the river was twice as wide as it is today in many points and was quite shallow. Large boats trying to get across the state never made it because of the underwater obstacles and the strong currents. So, by piloting the *Independence* riverboat from St. Louis to Franklin in 15 days, Captain John Nelson proved to other ship captains that the Missouri River was navigable.[144]

MAY
29 1915: The Kansas City Polytechnic Institute is launched.

The first junior college in Missouri came about due to an unusual situation that was causing overcrowding in Kansas City's schools. Many parents were sending their kids to a fifth year of high school to keep them close to home for another year before venturing off to college or the workforce. A meeting was held at the Knife and Fork Club in Kansas City to try and solve the problem of school overcrowding. The Institute's name was changed to Metropolitan Community College in 1975 to reflect the massive growth of the system throughout the greater Kansas City area.[145]

MAY 30

2020: Astronaut Robert Behnken blasts off on the first flight of the SpaceX Crew Dragon.

The Crew Dragon launched into orbit from Kennedy Space Center, making SpaceX the first privately made spaceship to carry passengers into space. Pattonville High School and Washington University graduate Behnken successfully docked the vehicle with the International Space Station the following day. On August 2nd, the trip came to an exciting conclusion when the crew splashed down in the waters off the coast of Florida.[146]

MAY 31

1995: The Missouri Mule is named Missouri's official state animal.

It's hard to believe that it took until 1995 for this to happen, because the mule had been synonymous with the Show-Me State for decades. The mule is the offspring of a female horse and a male donkey and became popular with early settlers due to its strength and endurance. Mules were first introduced into the state in 1820, just about the time Missouri became a state, and cemented their place in history when Governor Mel Carnahan signed a bill making the Missouri Mule the state animal.[147]

JUN 01 2018: Governor Eric Greitens resigns.

The charismatic former Navy Seal and Rhodes Scholar, who rose to prominence by positioning himself as a "political outsider," resigned after a brief time in office. Greitens shocked political forces in the Show-Me State by quickly making a name for himself while picking political fights on both sides of the aisle. He won legions of fans by calling out "Jefferson City corruption" and promising to clean up the "Mid-Missouri Swamp." However, the 56th governor of Missouri resigned following the revelation of an extramarital affair and calls for his impeachment over the illegal use of a donor list.[148]

JUN 02 1997: Red Chaney dies in Springfield.

Chaney was the entrepreneur who invented the drive-through window. For 38 years he operated Red's Giant Hamburg on Route 66. Chaney bought a gas station along the highway, which he expanded in 1947 by adding a restaurant near Chestnut Expressway and College Street. The restaurant included a window where the wait staff could pass food to hungry drivers. The new service was introduced to lure people off the road to grab a quick meal before resuming their trip. It was a hit with travelers and is now a staple of fast-food restaurants around the world.[149]

1875: Fasting and prayer begin to stop the
03 grasshopper invasion.

The "Year of the Locust" took on biblical proportions across Missouri for two straight years. Trillions of Rocky Mountain locusts descended on the Great Plains and devoured everything in their path, even blacking out the sky at times. Churches reported having daylong prayer services to stop the plague. Laura Ingalls Wilder described it in *On the Banks of Plum Creek*, where she said you could hear the insects devouring everything, and the houses were constantly full of the grasshoppers. The following year, the insects were gone and have never come back in such numbers again.[150]

1821: Missouri's first legislators meet in
04 St. Charles for the first time.

St. Charles was a bustling town by the time early state leaders picked the town to be the *temporary* capital of the 24th state. The legislators did not want the permanent seat of power to be in St. Louis, which had already been functioning as the territorial capital of the Louisiana Territory. Instead, they picked a desolate location along the banks of the Missouri River in the central part of the state to eventually be the capital. As work was beginning at Missouriopolis (later Jefferson City), the town once known as The Little Hills along the Boone's Lick Road stepped up. City leaders in St. Charles offered free meeting space for official state business, which helped bring even more civic engagement to the town. That first meeting of legislators took place on the second floor of a stately brick building along Main Street. The upstairs was divided into areas for the House and Senate, along with an office for Governor Alexander McNair, while a general store operated downstairs. St. Charles was the capital city for five years until official government operations were moved to Jefferson City in 1826.[151]

JUN 05 1888: The Democratic National Convention nominates Grover Cleveland in St. Louis.

It wasn't a big surprise, as President Cleveland had just finished his first four-year term as Commander in Chief, but there was still excitement in the air. The event was held inside the massive St. Louis Exposition and Music Hall, where thousands of delegates from around the country came to town for the nominating event. In a rare move, Cleveland was re-nominated by acclamation, which had not happened for a presidential candidate in nearly 50 years. Cleveland lost that race to Benjamin Harrison but ran again in 1892 and was victorious.[152]

JUN 06 1865: The Drake Constitution is ratified.

Charles Drake

Missouri lawmakers met at the St. Louis Mercantile Hall on January 6 to come up with a new constitution following the Civil War. The group met for three months and settled on what was called the "Drake Constitution." This new set of laws for Missouri had provisions that were at odds with the US Constitution. Among the most controversial was introduced by radical Charles Drake. It required citizens to take a "loyalty oath"—swearing that they had never supported the Confederacy—before they would be allowed to vote, work in any of several occupations, or sit on a jury.

This new constitution was extreme and became widely known as "The Draconian Constitution" because of the exclusions it contained. Two years after it was ratified by Missouri lawmakers, the US Supreme Court struck down the 1865 Constitution in the case of *Cummings v. State of Missouri* due to that "loyalty oath." It would take another 10 years before a replacement constitution was approved by legislators.[153]

07 1836: Missouri adds land with Platte Purchase.

The Platte Purchase is introduced by Senator Thomas Hart
Benton. The western border of Missouri was a straight line due north
from the Kansas City to the Iowa border for the first years of statehood.
However, early state leaders had interest in acquiring additional land
following the Indian Removal Act of 1830. Senator Benton's proposal
for acquisition included all the lands from the existing boundaries to
the eastern bank of the Missouri River. When President Martin Van
Buren approved the deal the following year, it added 3,149 square miles
to Missouri's northwest corner.[154]

JUN 08 1925: Birthday of the smallest man to play professional baseball, albeit only for a day.

Eddie Gaedel was thrust in the record books thanks to the marketing genius of St. Louis Browns' owner Bill Veeck. In the second game of a doubleheader, Gaedel was put into the game to pinch hit. At 3'7" tall, his strike zone was so small that it was nearly impossible for the pitcher to throw him a strike—so Gaedel walked. In fact, he had been told *not* to swing at any pitch. He had to borrow a uniform from the bat boy because there were no jerseys that would fit him. That bat boy is the current owner of the St. Louis Cardinals, Bill Dewitt.[155]

JUN 09 1913: Fire rages though the Springfield Square, again.

The heart of Springfield has been damaged twice over its lifetime. The blaze in 1913 destroyed nearly every building on the northeast corner of the square. The design of Springfield's square was unlike most others in that the roads entered at the sides, rather than the corners. That limited access to vehicles and pedestrians caused clogged streets as people flooded the area to see the blaze. The fire began in the Heer's store building and spread to the Queen City Bank, Nathan's Clothing Store, the A. W. Weaver Shoe Company, and several other buildings.[156]

JUN 10 · 1829: The town of Arrow Rock is founded as Philadelphia.

One of the earliest and most important cities in early Missouri history was founded under the name Philadelphia. The 50-acre site was laid out along the Missouri River near the navigational marker in the area known as the "Arrow Rock," which guided early travelers. The marker was so well-known in the area that dwellers began calling the small village Arrow Rock instead of Philadelphia, so it was renamed in 1833. The small town was the home of many of Missouri's early state leaders and dignitaries.[157]

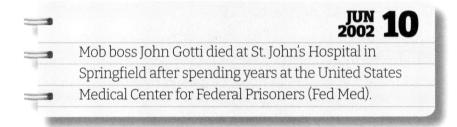

JUN 2002 10

Mob boss John Gotti died at St. John's Hospital in Springfield after spending years at the United States Medical Center for Federal Prisoners (Fed Med).

JUN 11 · 2010: *Winter's Bone* is released nationwide and becomes a huge hit.

The movie, based in small-town Missouri, made Jennifer Lawrence a star. The film was shot on location in areas around Hollister, using locals for many parts. It was released to rave reviews, and brought attention to some of the issues being faced by many families. Lawrence played a teenage girl who was protecting her family from being evicted while also dealing with an absentee father, poverty, and rampant drug use around her. The film received four Oscar nominations and won the Grand Jury Prize for Dramatic Film at the 2010 Sundance Film Festival.[158]

12 **2019: The St. Louis Blues win the Stanley Cup title by defeating the Boston Bruins.**

The St. Louis Blues hockey team was established in 1967 when the NHL added six teams during league expansion. The Blues found success early, appearing in the Stanley Cup Finals (and losing) in each of their first three seasons, but had spent nearly five decades coming up short. In the magical 2018–19 season, the Blues fired their head coach, were in last place midway through the season, put in their fourth-string goalie to start, and ran the table on the best teams in the NHL through the playoffs. The Blues finally won it all by defeating the Boston Bruins in the Stanley Cup Finals, 52 years after the club came into existence.[159]

JUN **13** **1948: The city of Bolivar is in the world spotlight as the statue Simon Bolivar arrives ahead of their celebration.**

The city in southwest Missouri was preparing to hold a Pan-American independence celebration in unity with Venezuela and in recognition of the town's namesake, Simon Bolivar. Bolivar was a Venezuelan revolutionary often compared to George Washington. So, Venezuela sent a statue of him to the city to mark the celebration, which was to be held on July 5. Both President Harry S Truman and Venezuelan President Romulo Gallegos were in Bolivar to unveil the statue, which has the caption:

The Government
and the people of Venezuela
To the Noble city which renders through its name,
a perpetual homage
To the memory of the liberator
SIMON BOLIVAR
July 5th 1948[160]

14 1965: The Beatles release the song, "Kansas City."

"Kansas City" was written by Jerry Lieber and Mike Stoller 13 years prior to the Beatles' release. Neither of the authors had ever been to Kansas City, but were so inspired by the works of Kansas City blues legend Big Joe Turner that they felt compelled to write it. It first became a hit in 1952 when Little Willie Littlefield released the song under the title, "K.C. Lovin." The hit was recorded again by Wilbert Harrison and hit number one on the Billboard charts. In 2004, the city of Kansas City made "Kansas City" its official song.[161]

JUN 1990 **14**

The 90th US Open golf tournament begins. Missourian Hale Irwin won the four-day event at the age of 45, making him the oldest US Open champion ever.

15 1947: The first televised golf match in history takes place in Missouri.

Golf history was made at the St. Louis Country Club as the US Open was televised on KSD-TV. Some of the biggest names in golf came to St. Louis to play in the prestigious tournament at the same time that broadcast technology was making live sporting events possible. The match was only seen in the St. Louis area, as the first nationally televised golf match was still six years away, at the World Championship of Golf tournament. Ironically, the same man—Lew Worsham—was the winner of both the 1947 US Open and the 1953 World Championship of Golf.[162]

JUN 16 — 1989: The crinoid becomes the official state fossil, thanks to Lee's Summit students.

Crinoids are the fossilized remains of prehistoric sea lilies, which are like sand dollars, that lived in the oceans that covered the US hundreds of millions of years ago. These fossils came into the news after a group of students from the school in the Kansas City area worked through the legislative process to make them a part of state history. These fossils can still be found, proving that Missouri was once a place at the bottom of the sea.[163]

JUN 17 — 1933: The Union Station Massacre rocks Kansas City.

In the span of 30 seconds, one of the most violent attacks on law enforcement took place in broad daylight. Multiple gunmen attempted to free convict Frank Nash as he was being transported. The criminals opened fire on the officers with machine guns. Four officers were killed in the shootout, along with Nash. Notorious criminal Charles "Pretty Boy" Floyd and Adam Richetti were named by the FBI as the gunmen.

Pretty Boy Floyd was later killed in Ohio, while Richetti was put to death in the gas chamber at the State Pen in Jefferson City.[164]

JUN 1946 17

The first cellular phone service in history debuts in St. Louis.

1808: City of Sainte Genevieve, the oldest city in the state, is incorporated.

The first permanent settlement in what would become Missouri was established on the banks of the Mississippi River. Although the exact date that settlers set up an official village is debatable, most historians believe it was around 1735. Many of the early families came across the river from communities in Illinois to farm the fertile land. Once the Louisiana Purchase was completed, the area became even more valuable to the emerging United States throughout the 1800s. The first settlement did move at one point, as constant flooding forced early families to relocate to higher ground in 1785.[165]

JUN 1949 18

Garroway at Large debuts on NBC. Dave Garroway, a University City native and Washington University graduate, was later the first host of The *Today Show*.

JUN 19   1929: 7-Up is introduced as Bib-Label Lithiated Lemon-Lime Soda.

What's in a name? When it comes to soda, a lot. Mid-Missouri native Charles Leiper Grigg was a soft drink icon. He moved to St. Louis from his hometown of Montgomery City to begin his career at a beverage company, where he came up with the drink, "Whistle." He left that company to come up with his newest concoction, which originally contained lithium, a mood-stabilizing drug. The name was later changed to 7-Up when it was reintroduced on June 23, 1936. The reason for the name is still a mystery, because Grigg never explained why he chose to call the beverage 7-Up.[166]

JUN 20   1985: Northeast Missouri State University is designated as Missouri's premier statewide public liberal arts and sciences university.

The college in Kirksville dates to 1867, when it opened as Missouri Normal School and Commercial College. The name of the school changed several times as it grew and its mission evolved. In 1870, the college became Missouri's first state-supported school whose primary purpose was educating future teachers. The name was changed again to Truman State in 1996, and it has since grown to be one of the top-ranked regional universities in the Midwest.[167]

JUN 21   1949: The Fairground Park riot rattles St. Louis.

A tragic day in Missouri history boils out of control after Black children are legally allowed to use the Fairground Park pool along with white children. A 1949 federal ruling paved the way for public facilities to be integrated. The white and Black kids were swimming peacefully together in the once "whites-only" pool when a mob of citizens descended on the area, yelling at the African American children. Throughout the following days, tensions continued to boil. Mayor Joseph Darst eventually ordered pools to be segregated until a solution could be found.[168]

JUN 22   1874: Doctor Andrew Still founds Osteopathic Medicine.

Andrew Taylor Still moved with his family to Missouri shortly after the Civil War, and he began treating sick people at no charge with a theory of medicine he had devised. Dr. Still relied less on drugs and more on treating the whole person—mind, body, and spirit—to promote healing. He called this medical philosophy "osteopathy." His practice in Kirksville grew rapidly, and he eventually opened a school to teach his methods called the American School of Osteopathy, which was later renamed as A. T. Still University. Today, osteopathy is one of the fastest-growing health professions around the world.[169]

JUN 2017 22

Jayson Tatum is drafted by the Boston Celtics with the third overall pick in the NBA Draft. The Chaminade College Prep standout followed in the steps of another Chaminade star, Bradley Beal, who was also drafted third in the 2012 draft by the Washington Wizards.

JUN 23 1966: H. W. Allen applies for a patent for the compound hunting bow.

Holless Wilbur Allen was living in Kansas City in the early 1960s amid a growing interest in bow hunting across the United States. Allen liked the outdoors, and he also like to tinker. So, devised a way to take a primitive bow, then attach standard pulleys to it to shoot arrows faster and longer than anything seen before. His idea revolutionized the archery industry, and his patent was granted three years later. He spent his later years in Billings, Missouri, and was inducted into the Archery Hall of Fame.[170]

JUN 24 1876: Forest Park officially opens to the public.

It's hard to believe, but at one point, the idea of opening Forest Park in St. Louis was controversial. The idea for a massive city park came about in response to a lack of green space and the pollution issues in the city. A large tract of land west of the city was chosen to purchase, which was approved by the Missouri legislature in 1872. Protestors believed that the park was too far from the city and was destined to be a playground for wealthy residents who had the ability

JUN 1992 24

One of Mizzou's all-time greats, Anthony Peeler, is picked 15th overall in the NBA draft by the Los Angeles Lakers. The Kansas City Paseo High graduate was a high school McDonald's All-American, collegiate All-American, and NBA star, playing 13 seasons as a pro.

and means to travel to the park, so they wanted lawmakers who supported it to resign. On opening day, an estimated 50,000 residents came to the park for the celebrations. Today, Forest Park remains one of the largest city parks in the world, with millions of annual visitors.[171]

JUN 25 1989: The St. Louis Walk of Fame on Delmar Boulevard is dedicated.

Delmar Boulevard, or the Delmar Loop, has been called "One of Ten Great Streets in America." It is the place where the cool people hang out in the coolest shops in University City. One reason it has become so hip is the St. Louis Walk of Fame, which honors notable people who are either from St. Louis or spent their creative years in the area. On that first day of induction the icons were recognized, including Chuck Berry, Katherine Dunham, James Eads, T.S. Eliot, Scott Joplin, Charles Lindbergh, Stan Musial, Vincent Price, Joseph Pulitzer, and Tennessee Williams.[172]

JUN 26 2000: World leaders and scientists cheer the announcement that the human genome had been mapped primarily at Washington University.

The ambitious, 13-year project was completed three years ahead of schedule, as much of the scientific work of the Human Genome Project was done at the Genome Sequencing Center at Washington University School of Medicine. President Bill Clinton said of the achievement, "Without a doubt, this is the most important, most wondrous map ever produced by humankind." Researchers claimed that the accomplishment was greater than landing a man on the moon and that it gave scientists the blueprints for how to treat and diagnose nearly all diseases in the future.[173]

JUN 2006 26

The Elks Lodge collapses in Clinton as several dozen members of the club are having dinner. Only one person, the president of the club, died.

JUN 27 **1993: The Mississippi River in St. Louis rises above flood stage, where it stays for 147 days.**

The Mississippi River went above flood stage for the second time in 1993 and stayed there for the next five months. In the first weeks of the flood, the waters were contained mostly to farmland. However, the crest on August 1 made for a satellite image that showed a river that was miles wide and looked more like a massive lake. The Great Flood of '93 finally came to an end in St. Louis on September 13, when the waters dipped below flood stage in front of the Gateway Arch.[174]

JUN 28 **2020: The McCloskeys make headlines with guns drawn in front of their home.**

Protestors marching through a gated community in the Central West End of St. Louis were met by homeowners Mark and Patricia McCloskey, who came out of their home with guns drawn, telling protestors to get off the land. The incident led to charges against the couple, lawsuits over the picture, and St. Louis in the national spotlight over debates about gun rights and private property. The incident took on another life after they appeared at the Republican National Convention, after the story got the attention of President Donald Trump.[175]

29 1950: *The Game of Their Lives* World Cup upset.

The soccer match that many consider to be the greatest upset in World Cup history happened when the US team beat England in Brazil, 1-0. Five of the players on the American team hailed from St. Louis, with four of them from the Hill neighborhood, along with a coach. England was considered a favorite to win it all, while the Americans almost did not even field a team. All the players from that team were inducted into the National Soccer Hall of Fame and the story was made into the movie *The Game of Their Lives,* which was released in 2005.[176]

30 1949: "The Missouri Waltz" is adopted as official state song.

The song has become a part of Missouri lore, even though it started out with a thud. The waltz was written by Lee Edgar Settle of New Franklin and released in 1914, but practically nobody bought it and it nearly slipped into obscurity. It eventually found its footing and sold six million copies in the following two decades. The rumor was that Harry S Truman was fond of the song, so the state legislature pushed for it to be the state's theme song, only to find out later that Truman actually disliked it.[177]

JUL 01 — 1973: UMKC Medical School residency program begins.

The medical school in Kansas City began in 1971 with only a handful of students. It has grown into a top-notch medical school with a unique program that takes six years to complete, as students are accepted right out of high school. When the medical school began, only 18 students took part in the medical curriculum. Only nine were a part of that first class of graduates, and only three took part in the residency program at Kansas City General Hospital.[178]

JUL 02 — 1991: Guns N' Roses Riot ensues at Riverport Amphitheater.

Riverport Amphitheater in Maryland Heights had recently opened when one of the biggest names in rock and roll came to town. Guns N' Roses had a reputation that preceded them as the "most dangerous band in the world." When the band began to play the song, "Rocket Queen," an unauthorized photographer got the attention of lead singer Axl Rose. Rose yelled for security to take the man's camera, but they didn't act fast enough, so the lead singer jumped into the crowd for a brief scuffle as the band continued playing. When Axl got back on stage, he announced the concert was over, and the band walked off the stage. The crowd erupted by throwing practically everything that wasn't bolted down at the stage, and a full-scale riot ensued. In the end, 60 were injured, several were arrested, and Rose was charged with several crimes, resulting in the band getting banned from St. Louis. But in 2017, Guns N' Roses did play St. Louis again . . . this time with no riot.[179]

JUL 1919 02

Missouri became the eleventh state to ratify the 19th Amendment, granting suffrage to women.

JUL 03 — 1981: First VP Fair kicks off in St. Louis.

The Gateway Arch was the centerpiece of a massive celebration designed to showcase St. Louis to the world on Independence Day. Businessman Robert Hermann helped organize the initial festival with the help of other influential residents and 1,000 volunteers. "America's Biggest Birthday Party" was an enormous success, with about 1.5 million people attending the three-day event on the Arch grounds. The name was changed in 1994 to Fair Saint Louis.[180]

JUL 04 — 1826: Death of Thomas Jefferson.

If it had not been for President Jefferson, there likely would be no state of Missouri, and there certainly wouldn't be a University of Missouri like we know it. In fact, his impact is so profound that his original tombstone lies in the middle of the campus.

Jefferson was precise about his tombstone, which consists of a six-foot-tall granite obelisk, a granite base with his dates of birth and death, and a plaque with the personally chosen inscription:

Here was buried
Thomas Jefferson
Author of the Declaration of American
*   Independence*
of the Statute of Virginia for religious freedom
Father of the University of Virginia

The tombstone was originally erected at Monticello but was moved to Columbia in 1883, when it was granted to the university.[181]

JUL 05 — 1879: The namesake of the Davis Cup is born in St. Louis.

Dwight Davis was much more than just a star tennis player and the namesake of the Davis Cup. Yes, he did win the US National Doubles Championship three straight years while attending Harvard. And yes, he was the founder of the international tennis competition that bears his name. He was also a lawyer, businessman, city parks commissioner, and a man who got things done. That may be why he was on the cover of *Time Magazine* during World War I as he served as Secretary of War and the Governor-General of the Philippines, then later as a Major General during World War II. Any one of those accomplishments are career-worthy; they just happen to be wrapped up all in one remarkable man from Missouri.[182]

JUL 06 — 1929: Springfield Public Schools relax restrictions on teachers.

Teachers in schools across the country were once faced with regulations that women in other professions didn't have to abide by on the job, some of which are laughable today. Teachers organizations eventually began urging local schools to drop the restrictions, including the Springfield Public Schools. Finally, on this date, Superintendent H.P. Study made the formal announcement that "Springfield school teachers may bob their hair, dance, smoke, play cards and go to movies if they desire, without breaking any school regulations, and without disastrous effect until they begin neglecting their work."

JUL 07 **1928: Sliced bread is sold for the first time.**

A giant step forward in the baking industry put Missouri on the culinary map, as the Chillicothe Baking Company sold sliced bread for the very first time. The bakery didn't invent the machine, but was the first to sell bread that was sliced by the machine. The event was pretty much lost to history until 2001, when a journalist looking over old newspapers saw the headline in the *Chillicothe Constitution-Tribune*, "Sliced Bread Is Made Here." Further research proved it to be the first instance of sliced bread being sold to the masses. The State of Missouri now honors Sliced Bread Day every July 7.[183]

JUL 08 **1984: The Jacksons' Victory Tour wraps up its world debut in Kansas City.**

It seemed like an unlikely place to kick off a world tour, but the Jackson family picked Kansas City as location to launch one of the biggest concert tours in history. Michael Jackson and his family played to packed audiences estimated at 45,000 at Arrowhead Stadium for three straight nights, beginning on July 6. The Jacksons' "Victory Tour" included 55 concerts to an estimated two million live audience members, wrapping up five months later in Los Angeles.[184]

JUL 1992 08

Melrose Place debuts with a Missourian, Jack Wagner, in a starring role.

JUL 09 · 1878: Henry Tibbe gets a patent for his corn cob pipe.

Tibbe came to Washington, Missouri, from Holland and established a woodworking business. He got an unusual request from a local farmer for a pipe to be made from a corn cob. Tibbe used his expertise to craft an early version of the pipe, which became a hit with locals. Tibbe also found a way to coat the cob to keep the tobacco from going out when lit. He named his blossoming company, H. Tibbe, Son & Co and was granted a patent on the pipe design, which he named the Missouri Meerschaum.[185]

JUL 10 · 1981: A shooting death in the small town of Skidmore captivates the nation . . . because nobody would talk.

Ken McElroy was well-known in the town in far northwest Missouri, but not for the reasons one might hope—McElroy had been with charged with more than 20 serious crimes. He was finally convicted of attempted murder in 1980 after shooting a grocery store owner in the neck, but was out of jail while the case was being appealed. Someone, or some group, had had enough of his antics and shot McElroy to death. The shooting involved two guns and reportedly occurred in front of 46 witnesses, all of whom said they didn't see anything. Nobody was ever charged with the crime.[186]

JUL 11
2003: The Norton grape is named Missouri's state grape.

Missouri has Thomas Jefferson to thank for the Norton grape. Jefferson had tried for years to establish a vineyard near his plantation in Monticello, but all varieties of grapes failed until Dr. Daniel Norton introduced him to some vine cuttings that finally worked. Those grape offspring eventually came to Missouri and helped establish our state as the nation's second-largest wine producer before Prohibition. Today, Missouri has more than 130 vineyards, with the center of Missouri's wine country based in Hermann.[187]

JUL 1983 11

The Miss Universe pageant was held at the Kiel Center in St. Louis. Miss New Zealand, Lorraine Downes, won the title, with Miss USA, Julie Hayes, taking first runner-up.

JUL 12
2009: Major League Baseball All-Star Game festivities begin in St. Louis.

The 80th midseason classic was a showcase of the new Busch Stadium III. And for Missourians, there was plenty of home-state pride

JUL 1963 12

Stanley Durwood invents the multiplex theater design in Kansas City. The Parkway Theaters in the Ward Parkway Shopping Center was the first known complex to have multiple theaters at one location.

to go around. In the Home Run Derby on July 13, Missouri legends Albert Pujols and Ryan Howard took part. On game day, "The Star-Spangled Banner" was sung by Kennett's Sheryl Crow, while New Franklin's own Sara Evans sang "God Bless America" during the seventh-inning stretch. Numerous players and managers from the Royals and Cardinals were in the game, which just happened to be broadcast by St. Louisan Joe Buck.[188]

JUL 13

1925: Birthday of Western Air Express, which later became a part of TWA.

Western Air wasn't based in Missouri, but it ushered in the future of Trans World Airlines during the Golden Age of Aviation with a long history in Missouri. The TWA brand came into existence in 1930 with the forced merger of three airlines under one banner and the official name of Trans World Airlines. Shortly after the merger, in mid-1931, TWA moved its headquarters to Kansas City and planned to make Kansas City International Airport its primary American and international hub. That plan was later abandoned. Meanwhile, across the state, Lambert Airport in St. Louis became a hub for TWA in the 1980s.[189]

JUL 14

1953: The first US National Monument dedicated to a Black American is established.

George Washington Carver was born a slave, but he spent his entire life breaking barriers and making life better for everyone. It is hard to quantify the impact he had on society, but being the first African American to have a national monument dedicated in his honor shows a fraction of his legacy. Carver is credited with creating more than 300 by-products from peanuts and 150 other products from soybeans and sweet potatoes. His fame as a scientist, however, may be eclipsed by his impact on racial equality.[190]

George Washington Carver

JUL 1954 14

The hottest day in Missouri history.
The temperature reached 118°F in Warsaw and Union, Missouri. Warsaw also holds the record for the coldest recorded temperature in state history, −40 on Feb 13, 1905.

JUL 15 · 1959: The "Birdman of Alcatraz" is transferred to the Fed Med in Springfield.

Infamous inmate Robert Stroud was widely recognized as one of the most notorious criminals in American history, although he spent the bulk of his life behind bars. Stroud began his life of crime as a teenager and was convicted of murder before he turned 20. He quickly gained a reputation as a bad inmate, too, who constantly got into trouble with staff and fellow inmates. While in solitary confinement in Kansas, he found three injured birds and nursed them back to health. He later became a respected ornithologist who helped with research on injured and diseased birds, all while in prison. He was later transferred to Alcatraz, and his research privileges were taken from him after he was diagnosed as a psychopath. So, it was big news when he was in failing health and was transferred to the Medical Center for Federal Prisoners (Fed Med) in Springfield. He died there after spending four years in Missouri. The notorious inmate had a movie made about his life, *The Birdman of Alcatraz*, after spending 54 of his 73 years in prison.[191]

JUL 16 · 1911: Song and dance superstar Ginger Rogers is born in Independence.

Rogers grew up in Kansas City and became a huge star during the era known as the Golden Age of Hollywood. Although she was a trained singer and actress, her greatest fame came from dancing performances with Fred Astaire. Rogers starred in over 70 films during her 50-year film career, and even won an Academy Award in 1941 in the Best Actress category for her portrayal of Kitty Foyle in the movie of the same name.[192]

JUL 17 — 1981: The Hyatt Regency walkway collapse claims over 100 lives in Kansas City.

The 45-story hotel opened to much fanfare in 1980 as the tallest building at the time in the state of Missouri. Tragedy struck the following year during a party at the hotel, as 1,300 people packed the atrium to celebrate during one of their "tea dances." As the festivities were taking place, the fourth-floor walkway collapsed onto the second-floor walkway. One hundred and fourteen people were killed in the collapse, and 216 others were injured. At the time, it was the deadliest structural failure in American history, eclipsed only by the terror attacks of September 11, 2001.[193]

JUL 18 — 1867: Birthday of *Titanic* survivor Margaret Brown in Hannibal.

Brown had lived quite an exciting life before she ever set foot on the infamous sailing vessel. Margaret Tobin grew up in Hannibal before leaving for Colorado when she turned 18. There, she married Jim Brown, who eventually struck it rich in mining, making her a wealthy young woman. Her divorce settlement gave the socialite the money she needed to travel the world, which led to a ticket on the *Titanic*. Her fame was cemented after a Broadway production and movie called *The Unsinkable Molly Brown* were made about her life story. She was also portrayed by Kathy Bates in the 1997 blockbuster, *Titanic*.[194]

JUL 19

2018: A duck boat sinks during a storm on Table Rock Lake, drowning 17 people.

An evening ride on the Ride the Ducks boat excursion near Branson turned deadly when a severe storm swept across the lake, capsizing the boat with 31 people on board. Duck boats are amphibious vehicles that can drive on land while also being able to float like a boat, and were used previously by the military. The incident was one of the deadliest boating accidents in US history and led to multiple criminal charges, lawsuits, and changes to maritime laws.[195]

JUL 2007 19

Mad Men debuts on AMC, with Jon Hamm in the lead role. The John Burroughs and Mizzou grad played the iconic role of advertising executive Don Draper.

JUL 20

1933: Bonnie and Clyde get into a shootout in Platte City.

The legendary outlaws' infamous run from the law had several Missouri connections. Early in 1933, Clyde Barrow and Bonnie Parker got into a shootout in Joplin that ended with two officers dead. Then, in the summer of 1933, the couple, along with their gang, arrived north of Kansas City as the Federal Bureau of Investigation's manhunt was taking place. They checked into the Red Crown Tourist Court but aroused suspicion, leading to another shootout with police, with an estimated 168 bullets being fired. The couple escaped once again. They were eventually cornered in Louisiana on May 23, 1934, where they were shot and killed by police.[196]

JUL 1910 20

The Christian Endeavor Society of Missouri begins a campaign to ban all motion pictures that depicted kissing between nonrelatives.

JUL 21 · 1865: The first known quick-draw shootout takes place in Springfield.

A shootout in the town square is a common theme in western movies, and it all got started on the town square in downtown Springfield. The dispute between Wild Bill Hickok and Davis Tutt began over a reported gambling debt from a card game. Tutt took Hickok's watch as collateral, but Wild Bill became upset that his adversary was showing it off. That led to a duel where both men fired their guns. Tutt missed, Wild Bill did not. Tutt was killed after the bullet went through his chest. In a later trial, Wild Bill Hickok was found not guilty of manslaughter.[197]

JUL 2017 21

Ozark debuts on Netflix, with Lake of the Ozarks as the setting.

JUL 22 · 1875: Allen Percival Green is born in Jefferson City.

A.P. Green made Missouri famous for our clay, which he made into fire bricks. The bricks that he produced at the factory in Mexico, Missouri, were extremely valuable, particularly for the fact that they were fire-resistant. During its heyday, the factory produced brick for institutions around the country, including Cape Canaveral, while also helping in the efforts of both world wars. Green's legacy in Missouri continued when his grandson, Christopher "Kit" Bond, became a Missouri governor and later a US senator.[198]

JUL 2016 22

Presidential candidate Hillary Clinton picks Tim Kaine as her vice presidential running mate. Kaine attended Rockhurst High School in Kansas City and the University of Missouri-Columbia prior to his political career, in which he became a US senator in Virginia.

JUL 23 — 2009: Mark Buehrle pitches the 18th perfect game in Major League Baseball history.

The Francis Howell High School alum took the mound for the Chicago White Sox at US Cellular Field against the Tampa Bay Rays and made history. For nine innings, Buehrle retired every single batter without a single player making it to first base. His perfect streak lasted more than five innings into his next game, in which he broke the record for consecutive batters retired, at 45.[199]

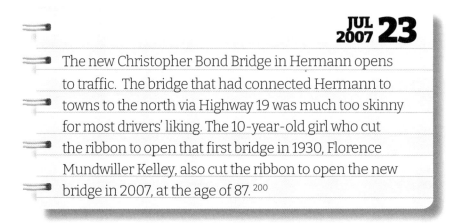

JUL 2007 23

The new Christopher Bond Bridge in Hermann opens to traffic. The bridge that had connected Hermann to towns to the north via Highway 19 was much too skinny for most drivers' liking. The 10-year-old girl who cut the ribbon to open that first bridge in 1930, Florence Mundwiller Kelley, also cut the ribbon to open the new bridge in 2007, at the age of 87.[200]

JUL 24 — 1983: George Brett's "pine tar" game becomes legendary.

The moment that George Brett charged out of the dugout will be forever etched in the minds of baseball fans. Brett just hit a two-run home run against the New York Yankees at Yankee Stadium in the ninth inning to give the Royals the lead. The Yankees challenged the play, claiming that the slugger had used too much pine tar on his bat. The umpires ruled that Brett had violated the rule and called him out. Brett ran onto the field for a heated exchange with the officiating crew. The Yankees won, until the Royals protested the decision. The American League president agreed with the Royals and ordered the game to be finished from the point of Brett's home run. This time, the Royals won, 5-4, 25 days after the original at-bat.[201]

1972: Vice presidential candidate Thomas Eagleton admits to having had shock treatments.

In the early 1970s, getting psychological help came with a stigma attached. Missouri Senator Thomas Eagleton had suffered from mental

health issues for years and sought help, which involved shock treatments by a physician. One week prior, Eagleton had been picked by George McGovern to be his running mate on the Democratic ticket against incumbent President Richard Nixon. Word leaked out about his "controversial treatments," forcing McGovern to ask him to withdraw from the

Thomas Eagleton

ticket. The admission did not impact his senatorial career, as he served in that capacity for Missouri until 1987.[202]

JUL 2003 25

University of Missouri-Rolla wins the 2,300-mile Solar Car Race. The students behind the Solar Miner IV dominated the American Solar Challenge race from Chicago to Los Angeles in a battle of vehicles powered only by the sun.

Downtown St. Joseph

JUL 26: 1843: The plat for a town 30 miles north of Kansas City is laid out. The new town is called St. Joseph.

A fur trader named Joseph Robidoux moved to the area around 1826 to set up a trading post for the American Fur Company at one of the final outposts on the frontier of the Wild West. The area began to grow following the Platte Purchase and as more settlers came to the area heading west. The village previously called Blacksnake Hills got the new name of St. Joseph, partly from Joseph Robidoux's first name and partly from the biblical Saint Joseph.[203]

JUL 27: 2003: Kansas City native Tom Watson cements his legacy as one of the greatest golfers of all time by winning the British Senior Open.

Watson was a star in high school at Pembroke-Country Day School, winning the Missouri State Amateur Championship four times. On the PGA Tour, he won eight major championships, but was especially dominant when playing in the British Open. He won that tournament five times, including the 112th British Open at Royal Birksdale in 1983, where he defeated fellow Missourian Hale Irwin by one stroke.

JUL 28 | 1881: A $5,000 reward is offered for the arrest of Jesse James.

Governor Thomas Crittenden had had enough of the reports of lawlessness coming from across the state regarding the James gang. Businesses were worried and citizens were in constant fear of being ambushed, so the governor was pushed into action. It didn't take long for Robert Ford, a longtime acquaintance of Jesse James, to act. Ford shot Jesse in the back in St. Joseph less than a year later and claimed the reward. Keep in mind that $5,000 in 1881 is worth about $127,000 in 2020, factoring in inflation.[204]

Thomas Crittenden

JUL 29 | 1904: The ice cream cone is invented at the St. Louis World's Fair.

Although there are disagreements about the actual date the cone was invented, this was the date that the International Association of Ice Cream Manufacturers recognize as official. Syrian immigrant Ernest Hamwi is credited with coming up with the idea. He used his wafer-like pastries as a holder for ice cream, which was the world's first version of the cone, although he called it the "World's Fair Cornucopia." Culinary historians claim that more foods were unveiled at the World's Fair than at any other event in history.[205]

JUL 30 · 1890: Baseball icon Casey Stengel is born in Kansas City.

Stengel was given the name Charles, but is better known by the nickname Casey from his hometown with the similar-sounding initials. He was a standout athlete at K.C. Central High before attending dental school at what became the University of Missouri–Kansas City. He got called up to the big leagues by the Brooklyn Dodgers in 1912 and played for several teams over the course of his career. He became the coach of the Yankees in 1949, not long after his playing career ended. He won ten pennants in his first twelve years as manager, including the first five.[206]

JUL 1994 30

Independence is hopping as dozens of politicians, along with throngs of media, converge on the town for President Bill Clinton's appearance. Clinton, along with First Lady Hillary Clinton, Vice President Al Gore and his wife, Tipper, appeared at the Truman Square to talk about health care policy.

JUL 31 · 1981: The last Corvette rolls off the production line in St. Louis.

Corvettes and St. Louis were a marriage that lasted nearly 30 years. The excitement began in 1953, when the *Post-Dispatch* reported that General Motors was finalizing plans to build a "plastic car" at a plant in the city. Later that year, on December 28, production of the Corvette was moved from Michigan to St. Louis. The first model year to roll off the line in St. Louis was the 1954 'Vette. For the next 27 years, America's favorite sports cars were built at that plant until the final, pearl-white, 1981 Corvette rolled out the doors.[207]

AUG 01 — **1988: *The Rush Limbaugh Show* debuts nationwide.**

The Cape Girardeau native was a big name in New York City on WABC radio in the late 1980s and became even more successful when he was introduced to a national audience. Limbaugh grew up in the Bootheel, where he learned the basics of radio broadcasting. He later had stints in Kansas City and Pittsburgh before WABC radio lured him to the Big Apple. The ratings for his nationally syndicated show skyrocketed in the early 1990s, as he became the highest-rated radio talk radio show host in the country. Limbaugh has also been inducted into the National Radio Hall of Fame and the National Association of Broadcasters Hall of Fame.[208]

AUG 02 — **1839: The *Missouri Whig and General Advertiser* newspaper begins printing.**

At the time, a newspaper hitting the press in Palmyra may not have seemed like that big of a deal. But nearly 200 years later, the paper was still in circulation as the longest continuously operating newspaper in Missouri. The paper's name was changed to the *Palmyra Spectator,* and it finally halted operations in October 2018.[209]

AUG 1937 02

A "funeral" service is held for streetcars in Springfield. The historic trolley cars were replaced with buses to modernize the city. The final trolley car parade took residents across the city one last time before they were retired.

AUG 03 — 1931: A patent is finalized for the car radio by William P. Lear.

One of our country's greatest inventors unveiled an invention that revolutionized the music production industry ... at least for a few decades. Though his name is most often associated with corporate jet airplanes, William Lear first made his mark in car radios with the patent for "Radio Apparatus: particularly the portable type used in automobiles." Lear was also the inventor of the eight-track tape cartridge and the founder of the LearJet Corporation, which revolutionized private air travel.[210]

AUG 04 — 1936: The "Fulton Flash" dominates the Berlin Olympics.

Helen Stephens is one of the greatest track and field athletes of all time and proved just how good she was during the 1936 Olympics. During those games, the Fulton native won gold medals for both the 100-meter dash and the 4×400-meter relay. These were the same games in which Jesse Owens made such a bold statement in the face of Adolf Hitler, and it wasn't much easier for Stephens. She was accused of being a man, and was forced to undergo an examination to prove she was female. Hitler later asked to meet her and had his picture taken with her. After her success in the Olympics, Stephens went on to play professional basketball with the All-American Red Heads.[211]

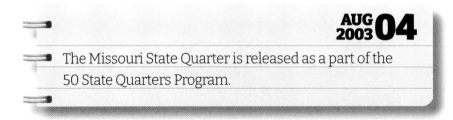

AUG 2003 04

The Missouri State Quarter is released as a part of the 50 State Quarters Program.

AUG 05 — 2001: The Hallmark Channel is founded.

Nothing says the holidays like Hallmark movies. So, it makes sense that a city like Kansas City, which makes Christmas so memorable, would also be the home of Hallmark Cards, the home base for those movies. Joyce Clyde (J.C.) Hall came to Kansas City in 1910 as an 18-year-old with big dreams, a couple of shoeboxes filled with cards, a strong work ethic, and little money. He and his brother Rollie expanded Hallmark's empire years later by inventing wrapping paper. The company didn't come up with the idea for the Hallmark Channel—it simply bought another smaller cable network, rebranded it, and the rest is Christmas history.[212]

AUG 1922 05

One of the deadliest train accidents in US history occurs near Sulphur Springs, as 34 people are killed when a Missouri Pacific train plows into the rear of another train.

AUG 06 — 1929: Bagnell Dam construction begins.

The dam construction project officially began, although timber harvesting had been taking place for months. When construction was completed less than two years later, the Osage River began backing up to form the Lake of the Ozarks. The water level rose about 1.5 feet per day, and it only took about 78 days for the massive

basin to fill in parts of Camden County, along with parts of Benton, Henry, Miller, and Morgan counties. Today, it is one of the largest recreational lakes in the United States, a top tourist destination in Missouri, and a setting for movies, and it is so iconic it is simply known by locals as the Lake.[213]

AUG 07 — 1861: James Eads is awarded a contract to build ironclad gunboats.

Before Eads designed the Eads Bridge, he made a name for himself "in" the river. The industrialist had been salvaging items from the bottom of the Mississippi River, thanks to early-model diving suits. Then the federal government awarded him a contract to build gunboats to help Union troops patrol the waters during the Civil War. His boats became the core of the US Army's Western Gunboat Flotilla and were key to several battles along the riverfront.[214]

AUG 08 — 1945: President Harry S. Truman signs the United Nations Charter.

The United States became the first nation to ratify the revolutionary document, paving the way for a worldwide organization geared toward achieving world peace. The United Nations officially came into existence on October 24 after the charter had been ratified by more than half of the countries involved. Supporters hoped that the charter would ensure peace following World War II, although the Cold War was waiting in the wings.[215]

AUG 09 — 2014: Shooting death of Michael Brown sparks protests.

The African American teenager was shot by Ferguson police officer Darren Wilson, sparking civil unrest first in Ferguson and then around St. Louis before demonstrations spread across the country. On November 24, a grand jury declined to charge the officer, sparking more protests. The US Justice Department later investigated the case and determined the officer acted within his rights, but the police department had displayed a historical pattern of racial bias, which was outlined in what became known as *The Ferguson Report*. Brown's death is also credited with sparking the Black Lives Matter movement.[216]

10 1821: The birthday of Missouri.

Missouri entered the Union as the 24th state in the United States of America. The plan for statehood, called the Missouri Compromise, was devised by Henry Clay, who proposed that Missouri enter as a slave state, while Maine entered as a free state. This agreement satisfied the will of existing states to expand the country, while keeping the balance of power stable in the United States at 12 slave and 12 free states. After contentious debate, supporters secured the votes from legislators, and on March 3, 1820, the House voted to approve

the Missouri Compromise, which also made all western territories north of Missouri's southern border "free" soil as well.

Missouri didn't become a state until 1821, but the first class of lawmakers and a constitution were already in place a year prior to statehood. The first Constitutional Convention took place in downtown St. Louis at the Mansion House Hotel, where it took only 38 days for state leaders to come up with a framework for the state. The constitution was adopted on July 19, 1820. The first elections in Missouri took place shortly thereafter, and Alexander McNair was elected Missouri's first governor. The Missouri General Assembly then met at the Missouri Hotel in St. Louis as the first session was gaveled into order on September 18, 1820.[217]

AUG 11 — 1949: General Omar Bradley is named the first chairman of the Joint Chiefs of Staff.

Omar Bradley

The Moberly native climbed the ranks of the military to be appointed the first chairman of the Joint Chiefs of Staff by President Harry S Truman. One year following his appointment, he was promoted to the prestigious rank of General of the Army, making him the fifth and last person to this point to achieve that honor. The US Army's M2 Bradley infantry fighting vehicle and M3 Bradley cavalry fighting vehicle are named after General Bradley.[218]

AUG 12 — 1927: Porter Wagoner is born in West Plains.

The man known as Mr. Grand Ole Opry first made a name for himself across southern Missouri before becoming one of the most famous country music stars of all time. Wagoner got his first real exposure on KWTO radio in Springfield and landed a recording contract soon after. Eighty-one of his singles landed on the Billboard charts between 1954 and 1983, including many with the woman he is credited with making a star, Dolly Parton. Wagoner and Parton were even named the Country Music Association's Duo of the Year for three years in a row. Wagoner was elected to the Country Music Hall of Fame in 2002.[219]

AUG 1817 12

Charles Lucas and Thomas Hart Benton agreed to their first duel on Bloody Island.

AUG 13 — 1956: First interstate highway work begins in St. Charles.

Three states claim to be the starting place of the interstate highway system, but it's hard to dispute Missouri's two claims. On June 29, 1956, President Eisenhower signed the Federal Aid Highway Act. Two weeks later, the first highway construction contract was awarded for a project in Laclede County on what is now Interstate 44. Even though the contract for the highway construction on Interstate 70 in St. Charles was signed later, the project was ready sooner and work began on August 13, making it officially the beginning of the nationwide system of interconnected highways.[220]

AUG 14 — 1971: Bob Gibson throws his first and only no-hitter.

Gibson signed with the St. Louis Cardinals in 1958 and became one of the most feared pitchers in Major League Baseball. Gibson overcame childhood health problems to play collegiate basketball at Creighton University, which led to a year of playing with the Harlem Globetrotters in 1957. But the excitement of playing alongside Wilt Chamberlain and Meadowlark Lemon wasn't enough. He signed with the Cardinals, played one year in the minors, and then began a professional career than landed him in the Baseball Hall of Fame in 1981. On the night of Gibson's only no-hitter, the team beat the Pittsburgh Pirates 11–0.[221]

AUG 1846 14

The "Cape Girardeau meteorite" captivates the country after the five-pound piece of space rock slams to the ground near the town.

AUG 15
1953: The Great Cobra Scare begins in Springfield.

The first of nearly a dozen cobras was found in a yard not far from a pet shop on St. Louis Street. At first there wasn't much concern, as the owner of the store denied that he was missing any cobras. But for two and a half months, more of the venomous snakes kept being spotted. Nobody knew for sure what happened until 35 years later, when a man finally came clean and admitted he let them loose. The man said the pet store owner wronged him, so he released a cage full of snakes he saw behind the pet store, thinking they were harmless. The incident left such an impression that the city seal of Springfield has a cobra to commemorate it.[222]

AUG 16
1868: Birthdate of "The Father of Physical Culture."

Bernarr Macfadden was famous while alive, and although he is relatively unknown today, his area of expertise is more popular than ever. Born in Mill Spring, he was an early proponent of the physical fitness movement. He published magazines about health, founded a utopian city based on healthful practices, and began the bodybuilding competitions that were precursors to the Mr. Olympia contests. Many people of his day thought that his methods of health were a sign of insanity, but

Bernarr Macfadden

millions of others bought into his teachings as he inspired a generation to live healthier lives.[223]

AUG 17 — 1936: Anheuser-Busch introduces Budweiser in cans.

The St. Louis brewery wasn't the first to package its product in cans, but the change in packaging certainly helped A-B to become a worldwide phenomenon. The American Can Company first came up with the idea of putting beer in cans in 1909, but Prohibition stalled the idea. Then, in January of 1935, the company mastered the process and partnered with tiny Gottfried Brewing Company in Virginia to sell beer in tin. Anheuser-Busch executives saw that consumers accepted the change, so they went full-speed ahead to adopt the practice. In a matter of two years, sales skyrocketed, making Budweiser one of the best-known brands in the world.[224]

AUG 18 — 1960: The first palm tree is planted inside the new "Climatron" at the Missouri Botanical Garden.

Architect R. Buckminster Fuller first came up with the idea of geodesic domes in the mid-1900s, and his patented design became a crowning achievement when the massive model was completed to replace the aging Palm House. The Climatron was designed by local architects with no interior support columns, to allow more light to penetrate the space. It opened to the public on October 1, 1960, and was so revolutionary that it was named one of the 100 most significant architectural achievements in United States history.[225]

AUG 19   1877: Reports of a "sea serpent" in the Mississippi River get the attention of scientists.

This wasn't just a fish story, as several eyewitnesses reported seeing the same thing. The headline in the *St. Louis Globe-Democrat* proclaimed that "An Aquatic Monster" was seen by several men who were sober and trustworthy while working on a levee. One man described it as 30 feet long with dark scales, a head like a dog, and a mouth like a pelican. Some of the workers speculated it might have been a giant alligator, while others surmised it might have been the devil. Scientists were intrigued, but nothing was ever found.[226]

AUG 20   1993: Coral Court Motel closes its doors.

The historic motel along Route 66 in Marlboro was legendary. The art-deco-style motel with glass block windows opened in 1941 about a mile west of St. Louis. It attracted families on vacation, outlaws looking to hide, and "lonely men" who valued the privacy of the individual bungalow rooms with attached garages. The No-Tell Motel was one of the few establishments in the city where you could rent a room for as short as four hours. When Route 66 was bypassed, business suffered. The small bungalows were knocked down in 1995, but the

motel remains on the National Register of Historic Places.[227]

AUG 2019 20

Major League Soccer announces that St. Louis has been awarded a team. The first female majority-owned team in Major League Soccer was headed by Carolyn Kindle Betz and named St. Louis City SC.

AUG 21

1813: Washington County is established.

The lead belt in Missouri has some of the oldest known history in the entire state and was one of the most important regions during the 1800s due to mining operations. Washington County sits right in the middle of that lead belt. The county was carved out of Sainte Genevieve County early in the 1800s before Missouri was even a state and is named after President George Washington.[228]

AUG 22

1876: The "Great Divorce" of St. Louis City and County becomes official.

As with most relationships, things were fine between the two entities until arguments arose over money and power. In the late 1800s, the city of St. Louis was the economic and political powerhouse of the region. City leaders and residents didn't like the fact that they were paying the bills for a county that was struggling, so they voted on a separation. It passed, thanks to some court intervention, and St. Louis declared its independence (while also taking some extra land in the divorce by expanding to 61 acres from 18.) Several initiatives have been pursued by area leaders to have the city re-enter the county, but thus far have failed to come to fruition.[229]

AUG 1948 22

Ulysses S. Grant marries Julia Dent at Hardscrabble.

AUG 23

2016: Robert Heinlein is inducted into Hall of Famous Missourians.

Heinlein is one of those rare Missourians who the masses may not recognize, but his loyal followers know everything about him. Known as the "Dean of Science Fiction Writers," he was born in Butler and moved to Kansas City, where he spent most of his childhood, graduating from Central High School. He turned to writing after a failed political run in California, which turned into a blessing in disguise. He churned out dozens of works, winning four Hugo Awards for his literature. Arguably his most famous work in 1959 also was turned into a blockbuster movie in 1997, *Starship Troopers*.[230]

AUG 24

1833: Columbia Female Academy, later known as Stephens College, is founded.

Columbia is known as one of the top college towns in America, and for good reason. The state's flagship university, the University of Missouri–Columbia, and Columbia College are both there. However, there was another school of higher education operating in Columbia for six years prior to Mizzou's founding. The Columbia Female Academy was born out of necessity; General Richard Gentry had five daughters who needed an education, so he helped organize the institution. That college later became Stephens Female College and is now the second-oldest women's college in the country that is still for females only.[231]

25 1900: New census shows St. Louis is the fourth-largest city in the US.

The total population of the city at the turn of the 20th century was 575,238, trailing only New York, Chicago, and Philadelphia. The city population peaked in 1950 with 856,796, and it was still the nation's eighth-largest city at that time. In that year, Kansas City was also on the list at number 20 with a population of 456,622. Both cities have fallen in the rankings, although Kansas City is now the largest city in Missouri, with 505,198 residents, and ranked 38th in the country, while St. Louis sits at 70th with 293,792.[232]

26 1873: First free Kindergarten in the US opens in Carondelet.

Susan Blow grew up in St. Louis but moved to Germany, where she studied the theories of Friedrich Froebel, the founder of Kindergarten. She saw the benefit for children and set out to bring this type of education to her hometown. Blow taught the children in the morning at the Des Peres School, while educating the teachers in the afternoon. Within ten years, every public school in St. Louis had added Kindergarten, which was also adopted by nearly every school district in the country in the following decades.[233]

Current River

AUG 27 — 1964: Ozark National Scenic Riverways are established as a national park.

One of the most beautiful stretches of wilderness in America was designated as a national park by an Act of Congress to forever protect the area. The Ozark National Scenic Riverways stretch across southern Missouri and include numerous pristine streams such as the Jacks Fork and Current rivers. The area now attracts an estimated 1.5 million tourists annually to enjoy the Missouri landscape just as it looked thousands of years ago. And with the national designation, the natural areas around Welch Spring, Big Spring, and Pulltite Spring will be unspoiled thousands of years from now as well.[234]

AUG 28 — 1820: Missouri's first state elections are held.

Although Missouri was still about a year away from becoming a state, elections had to be held to get government affairs in order. In that first election, voters had to pick a governor. Alexander McNair was elected as the first governor of Missouri by defeating William Clark of Lewis and Clark fame. Only about 10,000 people voted in that first election, with McNair getting 72 percent of the vote.[235]

AUG 29 1904: The Olympic Games officially begin in St. Louis.

The city had the world's attention during the summer of 1904 as it hosted not only the World's Fair, but also the Games of the III Olympiad on the campus of Washington University. Many countries refused to send athletes to the games, and travel issues also made it difficult for many competitors to get to Missouri. The games were historic, nonetheless. These were the first Olympics where the gold, silver, and bronze medal format was used. They were also the first Olympic Games to be held outside of Europe.[236]

AUG 30 1904: The Olympic Marathon debacle takes place.

Thirty-two runners from four nations took off from the starting line at Washington University, but only 14 finished. What happened in between is why some call it the worst race in history. Part of the problem was that the race started in the afternoon, when the temperature in St. Louis hit 90 degrees, so most runners failed to finish due to heat and dehydration. The course was also only about 25 miles, because the official marathon distance had yet to be standardized. The first man to cross the finish line was Fred Lorz, who promptly had his picture taken with Alice Roosevelt (daughter of President Theodore Roosevelt), but it was soon discovered he had stopped running at mile nine, hitched a ride back for about ten miles, and then run into the stadium. The true winner was Thomas Hicks, who had been given strychnine during the course to keep him going.[237]

Francis Field

31

1920: Marie Byrum of Hannibal becomes the first woman to vote following the ratification of the 19th Amendment.

Just five days after President Woodrow Wilson signed the groundbreaking law granting women the right to vote, Byrum cast her ballot. The 26-year-old woman had to walk several blocks to vote in the special election for the Hannibal City Council. However, Byrum wasn't the first woman to vote in American history. Wyoming had given women the right to vote a decade earlier. Interestingly, Wyoming also had the first female governor in US history, a woman named Nellie Tayloe Ross, who was from St. Joseph.[238]

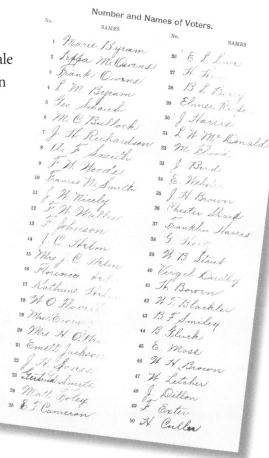

SEPTEMBER

SEP 01 1894: Union Station in St. Louis opens for business.

The first train pulled into the station at 1:45 a.m., ushering in a glamorous era and an unprecedented period of growth for the city of St. Louis. Architect Theodore Link's design, melding a train station with an extravagant grand hall, shocked people, especially with a price tag of $6.5 million dollars for such a building in the Midwest. It remained a focal point of the city, with the clock tower jutting into the skyline, until other types of transportation eventually replaced the railways. The last train pulled out in 1978, leaving the building vacant and in disrepair for nearly a decade.

Union Station got new life in 1985 when it re-opened as a magnificent shopping mall. Suddenly, the Grand Hall was bustling again, the hotel rooms were full, and tourists packed the facility for conventions, shopping, and nostalgia. Time took another toll, as people stopped coming in the early 2000s, until the station once again roared to life. An upscale hotel was added, an aquarium opened, the St. Louis Wheel began spinning, and one of St. Louis' most beloved landmarks was once again a crowd favorite by 2020.[239]

1850: Poet Eugene Field is born in St. Louis.

One of the most famous writers to call the Show-Me State home was born in Missouri but moved to New England after the death of his mother when he was only six. He returned to Missouri as a young adult and worked as a writer for the *St. Joseph Gazette* in 1875, the *Morning Journal* in St. Louis, and later as managing editor for the *Kansas City Times*. Even though Field didn't limit himself to poetry or to writing for children, he became known as the "Poet of Childhood" after he died in 1895 at the age of 45.[240]

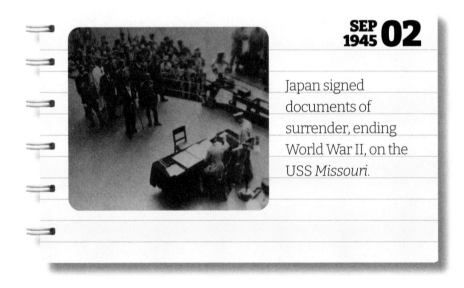

SEP 1945 02

Japan signed documents of surrender, ending World War II, on the USS *Missouri.*

SEP 03

1923: Cartoonist Mort Walker, author of *Beetle Bailey*, is born.

Walker grew up in Kansas City, where he graduated from Northeast High School. He attended the University of Missouri–Columbia, which had a major impact on his life. During college, he was drafted and sent to Camp Crowder in Neosho. All that background set the stage for the comic strip that made him famous. On the campus in Columbia there is even a restaurant called Mort's Grill, and there is a Beetle Bailey statue standing near the updated version of The Shack dining space on campus, which was often featured in his comics.[241]

SEP 1820 03

George Hearst was born near Sullivan. He graduated from the Franklin County Mining School, then headed to California in search of gold. His family's California home, known as Hearst Castle, now is a state park.

SEP 04

1813: Thomas Hart Benton gets into a gunfight with a future president.

Living in Tennessee at the time, Missouri forefather Benton got into a skirmish with Andrew Jackson at a Nashville tavern that led to a shootout. Both survived, and Benton later moved to Missouri. A mere four years later, Benton was involved in a pair of duels on Bloody Island. As for Benton and Jackson, both men were elected to the Senate in the early 1820s and were seated next to one another in the chamber, where they made up and renewed their friendship.[242]

SEP 1973 04

The Assemblies of God Graduate School opens in Springfield.

SEP 05 | 1906: The first forward pass in football history is thrown by a Saint Louis University quarterback.

Bradbury Robinson entered the record books when he made the pass against Carroll College. His first attempt was incomplete, which resulted in a turnover according to the rules at the time. Later, Robinson completed a 20-yard throw to teammate Jack Schneider that became the first touchdown pass. This history-making moment didn't happen because Billikens coach Eddie Cochems was revolutionary—it was more the fact that the rules had just changed and the Billikens played a game before other colleges in the country.[243]

SEP 1929 05

Workers begin clearing areas that became Lake of the Ozarks.

SEP 06 | 2009: Cyclists begin arriving in Missouri for final Tour of Missouri bicycle race.

Missouri was home to one of the most high-profile cycling races in the world for several years. It wasn't quite the Tour de France, but it was close in competition. The week-long event was gaining momentum heading into year three when funding was cut by the state. In that final year, racers took off for Stage One from St. Louis to Sainte Genevieve. Later stages took the riders through Cape Girardeau, then Farmington to Rolla, St. James to Jefferson City, and finally through Chillicothe, St. Joseph and ending in Kansas City.[244]

SEP 07   1959: The Shepherd of the Hills debuts on television.

Thanks to innovative technology, television station KYTV in Springfield was able to go on location and film newsworthy items for broadcast. Shortly after the station broadcast the opening of Table Rock Lake, the television crew decided to try their hand at filming a performance of *The Shepherd of the Hills*. The story is based on the 1907 book by Howard Bell Wright, which depicts families in the Ozark Mountains and their search for greater meaning in life. The book had been the basis for live performances in Branson and four films, including one in 1941 starring John Wayne.

SEP 2004 07 President George W. Bush holds a campaign rally at the Boone County Fairgrounds in Columbia, where he is flanked by saddles on each side as he speaks.

SEP 08   1998: Mark McGwire of the St. Louis Cardinals breaks baseball's home run record.

It seems nearly everyone in America, whether they were a baseball fan or not, was keeping track of the home run race between Mark McGwire and Sammy Sosa of the Chicago Cubs. The record of 61 home runs had stood since 1961, when it was set by Roger Maris. In 1998, destiny came calling. McGwire stepped into the batter's box in the fourth inning, ironically enough, facing the Cubs. He ripped the first pitch as a line drive into left field that barely cleared the wall, making it his shortest home run of the year. McGwire nearly missed first base, then touched them all for a raucous greeting at home plate by his teammates and son. Sosa even trotted in from the outfield as the two sluggers embraced, and play was stopped for 11 minutes for the celebration. McGwire finished the season with 70 home runs to Sosa's 66.[245]

SEP 09

1901: The first State Fair, held in Sedalia, opens.

The Missouri State Fair dates to the 1850s, when it was a small event held by the State Agricultural Society in Boonville. Legislators officially created the Missouri State Fair in

1899 after a request from the Missouri Swine Breeders Association for an event more formal and recognizable. When fair organizers decided to enlarge the annual event, they looked for a new location and settled

on Sedalia over other contenders, including Centralia, Chillicothe, Marshall, Mexico, and Moberly. The event is now one of the largest and most successful state fairs in the country.[246]

SEP 10

1959: *The Great St. Louis Bank Robbery* is released.

One of the most anticipated movies of the year, starring Steve McQueen, was based on an actual robbery that took place in south St. Louis. McQueen, also a native Missourian, was still relatively unknown at the time and starred as the getaway driver who was

hired to help pull off the robbery at Southwest Bank in 1953. The film had a unique twist: it was shot on location in St. Louis with some of the people who were caught up in the robbery playing themselves in the movie, including police officers, bank employees, and eyewitnesses.[247]

SEP 11 **2001: The terror attacks in New York City shut down most everything across Missouri.**

The situation in the hours and days after the attacks of 9/11 played out in Missouri much the same as in other cities. Air travel was halted, and many businesses closed as people rushed home to be with loved ones. People who were away from their homes had difficulty getting back, because there were no flights and rental cars were scarce. The American Express Classic was set to take place that weekend at Bellerive Country Club, forcing the PGA golfers to scramble to find transportation.

SEP 2016 11

The Munsters come to Macon. Actor Butch Patrick, who played Eddie Munster on the 1960s TV show, married Leila Murray in a ceremony in the mid-Missouri town.

SEP 12 **1930: The Grand National Bank becomes the first bank to open a drive-through window.**

Missouri has laid claim to many inventions and "firsts," including the ice cream cone, self-service gas station, and the drive-through restaurant. A banking institution along Grand Boulevard in St. Louis is also on that list for introducing the first known drive-through teller window. The idea came from Edmund Mays, owner of the Continental Building, which housed the bank. He came up with the idea so that a busy man "may transact his business without parking or leaving his machine." The outline of the teller window still exists in the bank's brick wall.[248]

2006: Dale Carnegie is inducted into the Hall of Famous Missourians.

Carnegie was a legendary author, educator, and self-development pioneer who transformed millions of lives through his best-selling books. He spent most of his childhood on a farm near Maryville, then moved to Warrensburg when he was 16. He continued his education at State Teacher's College in Warrensburg (now University of Central Missouri), where he excelled in public speaking. He took those skills to New York City around 1912 and began teaching classes in public speaking at a local YMCA, although he had trouble finding books to match his presentation materials. That's when he decided to write *How to Win Friends and Influence People.*

The book took the world by storm and sold more than 50 million copies. His entire philosophy on life was captured in the book, which made him one of the most famous personal development thought leaders of all time. He was even named one of the "100 Most Important Americans of the 20th Century" by *Life Magazine. Time Magazine* listed the self-help book at number 19 of their 100 Most Influential Books, while the Library of Congress named it the Seventh Most Influential Book in American History.[249]

SEP 1979 13

Benson debuts on ABC with St. Louis-born actor Robert Guillaume in the starring role. The versatile actor won Emmys for the character, and later found a new generation of fans by voicing animated characters like Rafiki in *The Lion King.*

Route 66 Birthplace courtesy Springfield CVB

SEP 14 | 1979: Bob Barker serves as Grand Marshal of Springfield's 150th Birthday Parade.

The Drury University alum and host of *The Price is Right* returned to Springfield for a massive sesquicentennial celebration. Barker made a name for himself on television by hosting *Truth or Consequences* for 20 years before becoming the host of The *Price is Right* in 1972. Barker attended Drury on a basketball scholarship after getting noticed by the coaches at nearby Springfield Central High School. He also worked at a Springfield radio station after a stint as a fighter pilot during World War II before heading off to bigger fame.[250]

Walter Williams

SEP 1908 14

The School of Journalism is founded at the University of Missouri-Columbia as the first "J-school" in the world. It was started by Walter Williams.

SEP 15

2017: A judge clears police officer Jason Stockley of murder in the shooting death of Anthony Lamar Smith.

The officer had been on trial for the death of Smith after a high-speed pursuit in St. Louis following a purported drug deal. Evidence presented to the court showed Stockley shooting into the car five times, killing the 24-year-old suspect. The circuit judge acquitted Stockley on the murder charges and armed criminal action. The ruling led to months of violent protests across St. Louis and in cities around the country.[251]

SEP 16

1984: *Miami Vice* debuts with the leading man from the Ozarks.

It may be hard to believe, but the biggest fashion icon of the 1980s was raised near the small town of Crane. Don Johnson split time between the family farm in southwest Missouri and his other childhood home in Kansas. Johnson was not only a star on the big screen, but also has several chart-topping songs to his name. That is no surprise to people who knew him growing up in the Ozarks, because both of his grandfathers were preachers and he often sang in church as a child.[252]

Debbye Turner (right)

SEP 1989 16

Miss Missouri Debbye Turner is crowned Miss America.

SEP 17 1866: Lincoln University welcomes its first class.

The first institution of higher education designed especially for freed African Americans in Missouri was established with the founding of Lincoln Institute in Jefferson City. The idea for such a school, which combined study and labor, came right after the Civil War from the soldiers and officers from the 62nd US Colored Infantry. The school began in an old frame building in Jefferson City and moved to its current location in 1870. College-level work began in 1877, and the four-year college of arts and sciences was added in 1934.[253]

SEP 18 1880: The *Kansas City Star* publishes its first edition.

At first, the new newspaper serving the Kansas City area was known as the *Evening Star* and hit the market amidst stiff competition. There were already several papers in the city, including the *Kansas City Times*, the *Kansas City Journal*, and the *Evening Mail*. The name of the paper was changed a few years later to the *Kansas City Star* as the publishing empire expanded to numerous other publications. Ernest Hemingway worked for a brief time at the paper and credits the editor with transforming his writing style and making him a more successful writer.[254]

SEP 19

1964: The Beatles spend a secret vacation in southern Missouri near Alton.

The Fab Four were winding down their US concert tour when they decided to get a little downtime before their final show in New York. After playing a massive concert in Dallas, they jumped onboard a small plane and headed to somewhere nobody could find them: the Ozark Mountains. The man who owned the plane also owned a ranch outside of Alton, where there were plenty of activities to help the band decompress. The British Invasion of southern Missouri lasted about 36 hours and included fishing, shooting, swimming, go-kart riding, and plenty of relaxing. The Beatles eventually made their way to New York for the concert on September 20, which turned out to be their final full concert tour in the US.[255]

SEP 20

1996: Sheryl Crow's song, "If It Makes You Happy," hits number one.

The Kennett native was on top of the world after her single became one of the anthems of 1996. Crow's Missouri roots run deep. She was raised in the Bootheel, graduated from Mizzou, and taught school at Kellison Elementary School in Fenton. During the evenings, she sang in a local band before venturing off to Hollywood. Several years after singing backup for stars like Rod Stewart and Michael Jackson, she became a star in her own right in 1993 with *Tuesday Night Music Club*. The album was a smash hit and included the song, "All I Wanna Do."[256]

SEP 2016 20

One of the most critically acclaimed TV shows of the 21st century debuts with a St. Louisan as a star. Sterling K. Brown portrayed Randall Pearson in the NBC drama *This Is Us*. The role won the Mary Institute and St. Louis Country Day School graduate numerous awards and led to a big-screen role in *Black Panther*.

SEP 21 1946: Benson Ford comes to Missouri for dedication of new Ford plant.

Henry Ford's 29-year-old grandson made the trip to St. Louis to formally dedicate the massive new automobile plant near Lambert Airport. The factory was a big step forward in keeping Missouri one of the largest automobile manufacturing states in the country, with St. Louis second only to Detroit in total production in the 1960s. The area where the plant was built didn't even have a name at the time; residents wanted to call it "Motorville," but decided on the name Hazelwood in 1949.[257]

SEP 2018 21

- President Donald Trump speaks at a rally at the JQH Arena on the campus of Missouri State University in Springfield.
- His "Make America Great Again" rally drew tens of thousands of people, who waited for hours outside.

SEP 22 1954: Missouri State Penitentiary inmates riot.

Tensions at the State Pen boiled over, following prison riots across the country over, the preceding months. Two inmates who pretended to be sick overpowered the guards, stole the gate keys, and let fellow inmates loose. Numerous fires were set as windows and furniture were smashed. By the time the riots were controlled, four inmates were dead and more than 50 others were injured, along with four officers. None of the inmates escaped, but the riots caused more than $5 million in damage. Governor Phil Donnelly ordered officers to comb the prison and confiscate all weapons and contraband they could find.[258]

1912: Theodore Roosevelt's whistle-stop campaign hits multiple Missouri towns.

After deciding not to run for another term in 1908, Roosevelt became disillusioned with the man he had supported for president, William Howard Taft, so he decided to run again in 1912. Roosevelt formed a new party called the Bull Moose Party to counter the

Republican Party, and hit the campaign trail to build support. His train pulled into Liberal, Missouri at 11:25 a.m. for his visit of the day in Missouri. He spoke to several hundred people before continuing to Lamar, Ash Grove, and then Springfield, where he gave a speech at Drury College. He then made appearances in front of several thousand people each in Aurora and Monett. He made an unscheduled stop in Carthage before his final event of the day at 7 p.m., where tens of thousands of supporters packed the st reets in Joplin. Woodrow Wilson won the election in a landslide, with Roosevelt and Taft trailing far behind.[259]

1987: The state of Missouri hires a consultant to explore the development of high-speed rail between Kansas City and St. Louis.

The idea of high-speed trains had been around for years, so the Missouri Highway and Transportation Department decided to see if the idea would work across the middle of the state. Amtrak passenger trains had a top speed of 79 miles per hour, while the trains under consideration could hit 170. The idea was later rejected. A similar idea called the Hyperloop was proposed in 2017. The Missouri route was a finalist but was not chosen for the magnet-levitated train project.[260]

SEP 25

2013: Astronaut Mike Hopkins launches in the Russian Soyuz headed for the Space Station.

Long before Hopkins was one of the most high-profile astronauts with NASA, he was a boy from small-town Missouri. He was born in Lebanon on December 28, 1968, then grew up on a farm near Richland and was a star football player at School of the Osage. The highly decorated astronaut also took part in the first mission to the International Space Station on board the SpaceX Crew Dragon, where he became one of the first members of the newly formed United States Space Force.[261]

SEP 26

1984: Bass Pro Shops breaks ground for new facility at Campbell and Sunshine.

Bass Pro Shops grew from humble beginnings into one of the largest businesses in America. It began in 1972, when Johnny Morris started selling fishing supplies inside his father's liquor store, Brown Derby. The small business eventually became more popular than his father's business, so the younger Morris knew it was time to expand. Now the store occupies more than 500,000 square feet and is one of the biggest tourist attractions in Missouri.[262]

SEP 27 — 1864: "Bloody Bill" Anderson's Centralia Massacre.

One of the most heinous incidents from the Civil War took place as William T. "Bloody Bill" Anderson's band of guerillas stopped a train in the town of Centralia in mid-Missouri. Anderson and his men shot 22 unarmed Union soldiers and then set fire to the train car. The lone Union survivor even reported that many of his comrades had been scalped. Missouri became notorious for these Confederate guerrilla fighters roaming the state, trying to force Missouri into alignment with Southern pro-slavery states.[263]

SEP 28 — 1953: Bobby Greenlease is kidnapped from school in Hyde Park.

The six-year-old boy was a student at Notre Dame de Sion school in Kansas City. That day, Bonnie Heady walked into the school and said she was a relative and needed to take Bobby because his mother had suffered a heart attack. Heady was part of a plot, along with Carl Hall, to kidnap the boy and get his parents to pay to get him back, although they killed the boy shortly after taking him. Bobby's father was the wealthy owner of Cadillac dealerships across the Midwest. He paid the largest ransom in American history at the time, $600,000, which would be worth around $6 million in 2020. Hall and Heady were captured, sentenced, and executed just months later at the Missouri State Penitentiary, where they gave each other a kiss before entering the gas chamber together.[264]

SEP 1952 28

St. Louis Cardinals legend Stan Musial makes an appearance as a pitcher. It was his first and only pitching appearance in the major leagues.

29 1963: Stan Musial Day in St. Louis.

The "Greatest Cardinal of All Time" was honored by the city as he played his final game. In that game, he went out with a bang by getting his 3,629th and 3,630th hits. Musial spent his entire 23-year career with the Cardinals and was inducted into the Major League Baseball Hall of Fame in 1969.

30 1970: Springfield is rocked in the middle of the night by a truck explosion.

A sniper shot a truck carrying about 20 tons of dynamite down Interstate 44, blasting a massive hole in the highway and rattling windows for miles. The blast near the Highway N/T exit west of town left a hole more than 20 feet deep and 50 feet wide. The truck driver was killed, and two men and a woman were arrested for the crime. The investigation showed it stemmed from a union dispute; the shooter was on strike against the trucking company that was targeted.[265]

SEP 1865 30

Cross-state train service begins as the Pacific Railroad locomotive goes from St. Louis to Kansas City for the first time.

OCTOBER

1812: The first meeting of the general assembly of the Missouri Territory took place.

The area known as the Louisiana Territory had been renamed earlier that year, on June 4, to end confusion between the large area acquired from France in the Louisiana Purchase and the newly admitted state, Louisiana. Legislators agreed on the name Missouri Territory with St. Louis as its capital and met for the first time to organize it further. At that first meeting, the five original counties in Missouri were established. They included St. Louis, St. Charles, Sainte Genevieve, Cape Girardeau, and New Madrid.[266]

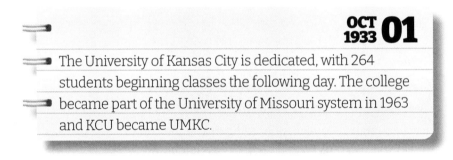

OCT 1933 01

The University of Kansas City is dedicated, with 264 students beginning classes the following day. The college became part of the University of Missouri system in 1963 and KCU became UMKC.

OCT 02 **2008: Joe Biden and Sarah Palin battle in a vice presidential debate at Washington University.**

The highest-rated vice presidential debate of all time took place on the campus of Washington University, as an estimated 70 million people watched the two go toe-to-toe. That debate pitted Palin, the governor of Alaska and first woman on the Republican ticket, against Biden, the 36-year veteran of the Senate.[267]

OCT 03   2014: The movie *Gone Girl* is released nationwide.

It's not very often that a box officer thriller showcases a small town in Missouri, so it was big news when the film hit theaters. The film was based on the 2012 book of the same name by Kansas City native Gillian Flynn. Hollywood stars like Ben Affleck, Neil Patrick Harris, Tyler Perry, and Rosamund Pike came to Missouri, where they shot the film in various locations in the areas around Cape Girardeau. Although the town where the film was set, North Carthage, was fictional, many of the filming locations are places you can still visit today. The film was a major success, grossing $370 million at the box office.[268]

OCT 1999 03

Family Arena in St. Charles opens with John Mellencamp as the first concert headliner.

OCT 04   1918: Increasing cases of "Spanish Flu" are reported across the state.

The 1918 flu pandemic had a massive impact on Missouri and the rest of the country and killed millions around the world. Part of the problem was a lack of understanding of the virus, coupled with the virus being passed around as soldiers returned home from World War I. Although it is impossible to determine when the flu officially arrived in Missouri, people across the state were being told to avoid crowds, get rest, and avoid alcohol for weeks in advance. In response to the fast-spreading illness, all three of Missouri's medical schools—Washington University, Saint Louis University, and A. T. Still University—graduated their classes early to get more doctors into the workforce.

Frank James

OCT 05 — 1882: Frank James surrenders to the governor of Missouri and stands trial for robbery and murder.

Frank James was trying to leave his life of crime behind and settled in Nashville, Tennessee, under an assumed name. Six months after his brother Jesse James was killed, James came back to Missouri to come clean. He turned himself in to Governor Tom Crittenden, the same man who had put a bounty on Jesse's head. Frank James went on trial in both Missouri and Alabama, where he was acquitted in both states. He moved back to Missouri following his mother's death in 1911 and died on the family farm in Clay County four years later.[269]

OCT 1836 05

The Medical School at Saint Louis University is established; it is the oldest medical school in the state of Missouri.

OCT 06 — 1990: Astronaut Tom Akers lifted off on the first of his four Space Shuttle flights.

Akers grew up in Eminence before heading off for college at the University of Missouri-Rolla (now Missouri University of Science and Technology). He earned his bachelor's and master's degrees at the university before returning to his hometown to become a math teacher. But when an Air

Space shuttle Discovery

Force recruiter left brochures for the students, the teacher picked one up, and eventually found himself in the astronaut program. His first space flight was on Space Shuttle Discovery, where he was a mission specialist. He also flew on Endeavor and Atlantis before retiring from NASA in 1997.[270]

OCT 07 — 1954: The first of the Pruitt-Igoe homes are ready for families.

The idea for a large-scale urban housing project seemed like a great one. However, when it was put into practice, it turned into a living nightmare for thousands of families. The housing projects were designed to lift poor St. Louis residents out of horrible living conditions and into homes that would supply a sense of security. But as soon as families moved in, so did crime; the 11-story high-rises became prisons for poor families, who could not escape. It took only 20 years for the officials to realize the project was an abysmal failure, and all 33 buildings were imploded by 1976.[271]

08   2006: *Eloise: The Animated Series* debuts, displaying the work of St. Louis native Kay Thompson.

One of the most iconic book series for children, which revolves around the life of a young girl living in the penthouse in the Plaza Hotel, has roots in Missouri. Thompson grew up in St. Louis and based her books off her childhood imaginary best friend. The Eloise book series was later adapted for both TV and film, including the animated version.[272]

09   1944: Cardinals win Streetcar Series against Browns.

St. Louis' two professional baseball teams battled it out for bragging rights in the first and only all–St. Louis World Series in 1944. The St. Louis Cardinals entered the game as the National League champions, while the St. Louis Browns represented the American League. The Cardinals won the title four games to two in the third and final World Series to be played in a single stadium, as both teams called Sportsman's Park their home field.[273]

10 1937: The Ozarks Empire Fair begins its inaugural seven-day run.

The fair had been around since the early 1900s as a traveling exhibit of crafts and other household items. Fair organizers decided they needed a permanent location to expand the fair and settled on a spot near the Springfield Zoo. The Greater Ozarks Empire District Free Fair opened and is still running, although significant changes have taken place. The fair was moved from October due to cold weather one year and because students could not attend during the day due to school. The admission fees were added in the 1940s.[274]

OCT 1926 **10**

St. Louis Cardinals win their first World Series title.

11 1991: Redd Foxx dies of a heart attack on the set of *The Royal Family*.

The actor from St. Louis had one of the most storied careers of any comedian in history. His breakout role came in 1972 with *Sanford and Son,* in which he played lovable junk dealer Fred Sanford. He became one of the only performers ever to have the lead role in a TV show on each of the big three networks, *Sanford and Son* on NBC, *The Royal Family* on CBS, and *The Redd Foxx Comedy Hour* on ABC. Fred Sanford of *Sanford and Son* was ranked No. 42 on TV Guide's list of the "50 Greatest TV Dads of All Time."[275]

OCT 1910 **11**

Theodore Roosevelt becomes the first president to ride in an airplane after taking off from St. Louis's Kinloch Field. It happened after he left office.

OCT 12
1964: Dr. Martin Luther King Jr. delivers a major speech in Missouri.

Dr. Martin Luther King Jr. spoke to thousands of students, faculty, and staff at Saint Louis University inside the West Pine Gymnasium. That historic speech came two days before King was awarded the 1964 Nobel Peace Prize. He gave a total of four speeches in St. Louis, including his first in 1957 at the Kiel Center when he was only 28 years old.[276]

OCT 13
1887: The Priests of Pallas parade debuts in Kansas City.

The week-long festival was a remarkable sight and attracted big names to the city for decades. Pallas was a pseudonym for the Greek goddess Athena, while the Priests' Den was the warehouse where the floats were staged. Crowds would gather to see the elaborate floats and the costumed performers. In the first year of the festival, the city's "elite residents" were invited to a ball to greet a dignitary attending the event. That VIP turned out to be President Grover Cleveland and his new, 21-year-old bride, Frances Folsom. The festival was held annually until 1912 and was the "must-attend" event of the year.[277]

OCT 14
1985: "Go crazy, folks, go crazy."

One of the most famous radio calls in baseball history happened when Cardinals shortstop Ozzie Smith hit a game-winning home run in the ninth inning of the fifth game of the National League Championship Series. Ozzie stepped into the batter's box in Busch Stadium against the Dodgers to bat left-handed. But in 3,009 career at-bats, he had never hit a home run from the left side. When he blasted the pitch over the right field wall, broadcaster Jack Buck uttered the words, "Smith corks one into right down the line . . . it may go. . . . Go crazy, folks, go crazy! It's a home run and the Cardinals have won the game."[278]

OCT 15 1969: Protests against the Vietnam War erupt during Moratorium Day.

College campuses across the state of Missouri were the epicenters for the "Moratorium to End the War in Vietnam." One of the biggest events took place at the University of Missouri–Columbia, where students and faculty left their classrooms to protest. Similar events happened at Washington University, Saint Louis University, and the University of Missouri-St. Louis. In Kansas City there were smaller protests reported on several campuses, although many protestors from Missouri crossed the state line to take part in a massive rally at the University of Kansas.[279]

OCT 16 2000: Governor Mel Carnahan dies in a plane crash near Hillsboro.

Governor Carnahan was in a heated battle for the US Senate with incumbent John Ashcroft when his plane went down in Jefferson County. When state leaders were unable to communicate with him, the State Disability Board met to swear in Lt. Gov. Roger Wilson as the acting governor at 2:25 a.m. Later, the bodies of Carnahan, his son, and a campaign aide were found, and Wilson became Missouri's 52nd governor. A memorial service was held four days later for the Elsinor native and attended by President Bill Clinton, who had been in St. Louis for a presidential debate when the crash happened. The Missouri Senate race suddenly became the focus of the nation. The election was only weeks away and it was too late for the Democrats to pick a new candidate, so party leaders urged his wife, Jean Carnahan, to fill the seat posthumously if he won. She reluctantly accepted and ran the final weeks of the campaign, while still mourning the loss of her husband and son. The deceased Governor won the election by two percentage points, and his widow served as senator for two years.[280]

OCT 17

1917: Search crews begin going through the rubble after the Kansas City Stockyards fire.

One day after a massive fire tore through the stockyards west of the city, firefighters were still putting water on the smoldering rubble and searching for evidence and bodies. The fire broke out the morning of October 16 at one of the largest stockyards in the world. Some 47,000 head of cattle were at the facility at the time, many of which burned in the blaze. After fighting the fire most of the day, firefighters finally had it under control after the inferno had destroyed an area equal to six city blocks. The stockyards were rebuilt, but they were wiped out again in the Flood of 1951 and closed for good in 1991.[281]

OCT 18

1914: First Mass takes place at the Cathedral Basilica of St. Louis.

The incredibly ornate structure was under construction for seven years before the first service was finally held. Ground was broken on the Roman Catholic cathedral in St. Louis' Central West End in 1907, but the plans for such a massive structure to accommodate the growing Catholic population in St. Louis took years to complete. It was initially called the St. Louis Cathedral, until Pope John Paul II appointed the superstructure a Basilica in 1997.[282]

OCT 1988 18

Roseanne debuts on ABC television with Affton native John Goodman in a starring role. His character, Dan Conner, was named one of "TV Guide's 50 Greatest TV Dads of All Time."

19

1990: *The White Palace* debuts in theaters.

The romantic drama starring Susan Sarandon and James Spader used St. Louis as a backdrop. The movie was based on the novel of the same name about the relationship of a young man and older woman who was working as a waitress. Although the film only grossed about $17 million at the box office, many St. Louisans have seen the movie purely to pick out the locations highlighted in the movie. The White

Knight Diner is still in business at 1801 Olive, while other locations like the Lemp Mansion and another mansion in Frontenac are still around.[283]

1803: The US Senate approves

OCT the Louisiana Purchase.

20

President Thomas Jefferson sent a treaty to the Senate earlier in the year, detailing his plan to purchase the huge swath of territory from France. The land included more than 800,000 acres of land—enough to double the size of the United States—including land that would become Missouri. Although Jefferson already had the deal in place, he insisted the Senate be involved because he could find nothing in the Constitution that allowed the new government to buy land. When all

was approved, St. Louis became the seat of government for the newly acquired area.[284]

Courtesy of William Morris

Ha Ha Tonka Mansion

OCT 21 — 1942: Ha Ha Tonka Mansion burns to the ground.

The beautiful mansion built on the cliffs high above the Niangua River caught fire in 1942, leaving behind the ruins that are still visible near Camdenton. The European-style castle was the dream of Robert Snyder Sr. of Kansas City, who had fallen in love with the area. Sparks from one of the chimneys caught the roof on fire and burned much of the mansion to the ground. The castle ruins and thousands of surrounding acres sat deserted until the state of Missouri decided to commemorate the area as Ha Ha Tonka State Park in 1978.[285]

OCT 22 — 2001: Video game enthusiasts line up at stores across the state as Grand Theft Auto 3 is released.

Television news crews in nearly every city reported on the long lines of people waiting, sometimes for days, for the stores to open so they could be the first to buy the 3D game. The game was set to be released weeks earlier but was delayed due to the attacks of September 11. Even though the producers of the game faced backlash for depictions of violence, it was the highest-selling game of 2001, with over two million units sold in the first four months.

OCT 23 — 1992: Nearly $1 million is stolen during a heist at the United Missouri Bank.

It is one of the most bizarre (and still unsolved) bank robberies in Missouri history, and there is still $847,000 out there somewhere. Two men wearing stocking masks and white overalls robbed a Brinks Security guard at the bank at 10 South Broadway in downtown St. Louis. The guard was pushing the money through a basement hallway when the gunman stopped him and tied him up in a building full of construction crews. A janitor later found tape, pantyhose, jumpsuits, and about $1,000 on the 13th floor. The security guard was cleared by police, as were the construction workers on site. Police never developed any solid leads on the case.[286]

OCT 24 — 1962: The Cuban Missile Crisis affects businesses and schools across Missouri.

Although the issues that led to the Cuban Missile Crisis happened more than 1,000 miles away, the impact on Missouri was felt immediately. President John F. Kennedy announced that launchpads for Soviet missiles had been found in Cuba, and schools began going over emergency plans in case of a nuclear attack. Four days prior, President Kennedy had canceled an appearance at the Westroads Shopping Center in St. Louis, claiming he was ill. That was actually the day the missile sites had been discovered, and the president was rushing back to Washington, DC for emergency meetings.[287]

OCT 25

1999: A plane crash claims the life of Springfield professional golfer Payne Stewart.

An eerie situation played out in the skies over middle America as a ghost plane streaked across the sky with no contact from anyone inside. The Learjet, carrying Payne Stewart, three other passengers, and two pilots, had taken off from Orlando en route to Dallas when it lost cabin pressure, causing all on board to lose consciousness. The jet eventually ran out of fuel and crashed in North Dakota. Stewart was one of the most beloved golfers on the PGA Tour and was ranked in the Top 10 of the Official World Golf rankings and third on the all-time money list when he died.[288]

Payne Stewart, Getty Images

OCT 26

1985: The infamous Don Denkinger game of the Interstate 70 series is played.

The 1985 World Series pitted the St. Louis Cardinals against the Kansas City Royals. The Cardinals led Game 6 1-0 going into the bottom of the ninth inning, when "The Call" changed the course of the series. An infield grounder by Royals leadoff hitter Jorge Orta turned into a base hit after umpire Don Denkinger got the call wrong, ruling Orta safe when images show he was out. The blown call was followed by a two-run rally in the bottom of the ninth by Kansas City, tying the series 3-3. Game 7 was a blowout as the Royals thumped the Cardinals 11-0 to win their first World Series title.[289]

OCT 1909 26

A massive crowd gathers on the Cape Girardeau riverfront as President William Howard Taft's flotilla arrives on the Mississippi River for a visit.

OCT 27

1838: Missouri's governor signs the "Mormon Extermination Order."

The Mormon War erupted in 1838 with clashes between residents and members of the Mormon church and culminated in an "Extermination Order" by Governor Lilburn Boggs. That order declared that all Mormons were to be driven out of the state or "exterminated." The group's approximately 15,000 followers were forced to move as Mormon leaders were jailed and their property was confiscated. Among those who left was a young man named Brigham Young. He later founded Salt Lake City and served as the first territorial governor of Utah.[290]

OCT 28

1965: The Gateway Arch is officially completed.

The final piece of stainless steel was put in place between the two giant legs to complete the Gateway Arch

in downtown St. Louis. It topped out at 630 feet, making it the tallest monument in the US. The final installation took longer than expected because of thermal expansion. The gap was smaller than expected, so the crews had to spray cool water on the legs to cause them to contract just enough for the triangular piece to slide into place. This was the culmination of a project that began back in 1947, when Eero Saarinen designed the monument to symbolize the Gateway to the West.[291]

OCT 2011 28

St. Louis Cardinals' David Freese wins the World Series MVP award after his stellar performance in the postseason. The Lafayette High School alum saved the season in Game 6 with his heroics, then hit another home run in Game 7 to help win the title.

OCT 29 — 1929: "Black Tuesday" stock market crash.

Many Missourians, especially in the growing cities, were experiencing a relatively stable lifestyle in the years leading up to the crash on Wall Street. But in the weeks and years after, life for many was never the same. Unemployment had hit nearly 25 percent of white Missourians by 1934, and more than 70 percent of Blacks. Afterward, "Hoovervilles" popped up in whatever empty space was available and remained in some areas for decades. In many smaller towns, economies were decimated. Farmers had fewer places to sell their crops as the ripple effect worked its way throughout the country.

OCT 30 — 1914: Kansas City's Union Station opens for business.

Union Station replaced the Union Depot, which had been called the "Jackson County Insane Asylum" due to its enormous size for the time. But growth in Kansas City called for something even larger, resulting in the Beaux Arts-style building that beautified the downtown area. In the Grand Hall, designer Jarvis Hunt went all-out, with three massive chandeliers and the clock that signified to many that the city was becoming a connecting point for older cities to the east and new growth to the west. The depot began to decline as rail traffic fell significantly, but the structure was renovated in 1996 to become an entertainment and cultural destination, with movie theaters, restaurants, science exhibits, and live performance areas.[292]

OCT 2008 30

Barack Obama holds one of the biggest political rallies in Missouri history on the Carnahan Quadrangle at the Mizzou campus in the days before his first presidential election.

OCT 31 1891: Mizzou plays Kansas in football for the first time.

When the University of Missouri and the University of Kansas met for the football game on that fall day, they had no idea it would become such a rivalry. The Jayhawks won the first meeting, 22-10. The teams played met annually in the early years, although not in 1918. The teams then began an uninterrupted, 93-year stretch of games that ended when the Tigers moved to the Southeastern Conference in 2011. The rivalry is still the second-most played rivalry in Division I football history, with 120 games. Mizzou leads the series 56-55-9. The teams will renew their rivalry beginning in 2025.[293]

OCT 1900 31

Keytesville's Cal Hubbard is born. The Missourian became the only man to be inducted into the Pro Football Hall of Fame and the Major League Baseball Hall of Fame.

NOV 01 — 1855: Gasconade River train disaster.

A tragic incident took place on the rail lines in Gasconade as a trip of celebration turned into disastrous crash. Rail lines had finally been established between St. Louis and Jefferson City, and a group of 600 riders and dignitaries boarded the train for the inaugural trip. Sadly, the bridge across the Gasconade River west of Hermann collapsed, sending the engine and many cars into the ravine below. An estimated 30 to 40 people died in the crash, including many well-known St. Louisans, as the first passenger car full of VIPs was crushed by the locomotive.[294]

NOV 02 — 1948: Harry S. Truman defeats Thomas E. Dewey for the US presidency.

It was perhaps the most famous election-day gaffe in history, made famous in Missouri. Early polls were not looking good for Missourian Harry S. Truman. Thomas Dewey was the favorite to win the presidency, and The *Chicago Tribune* had published an early edition of the paper with the headline, "DEWEY DEFEATS TRUMAN." The polls were wrong, and Truman rolled to victory that night, but it was too late to stop the press. The faulty edition of the paper ended up in the hands of Truman on November 3 as he was appearing at Union Station in St. Louis to celebrate his victory.

Courtesy Getty Images

NOV 03

1923: The Shrine Mosque is dedicated in Springfield.

The beautiful structure in downtown Springfield is one of the most recognizable structures in Missouri and has been host to numerous historic events. When construction was completed, the Abou Ben Adhem Shrine Mosque was the largest auditorium west of the Mississippi with the second-largest stage in the country, trailing only the Metropolitan Opera in New York City. The building was placed on the National Register of Historic Places in 1982.[295]

NOV 2007 03

Race car driver Carl Edwards of Columbia wins the NASCAR Busch Series Championship.

NOV 04

1979: The Iranian hostage siege begins, with Missourian Rocky Sickmann as one of the victims.

Marine Corps Sgt. Rodney "Rocky" Sickmann of Krakow was one of 52 Americans held hostage for 444 days in Iran. It began when an Iranian mob overtook the US embassy in Tehran, following President Jimmy Carter's decision to allow Iran's deposed dictator to get medical treatment in America. The crisis resulted in the deaths of eight military members, helped cost Carter the 1980 presidential election to Ronald Reagan, and started the TV show *Nightline*. Sickmann and the other hostages were freed on January 20, 1981 as the Washington High alum returned to Missouri and received a hero's welcome.[296]

1931: Gunfire erupts inside the Elms Hotel after 05 a botched robbery.

An attempted robbery at the upscale hotel in Excelsior Springs turned violent, with more than 40 shots fired inside the

lobby and veranda. The historic hotel near the famous springs was typically serene and has played host to presidents. But on this day, it was chaos as four men tried to rob the hotel, only to be confronted by police, ending in the massive gun battle. The robbers escaped and were later apprehended in Kansas City.[297]

NOV 1971 05

Former Redbird Mike Shannon is named as Jack Buck's partner on the St. Louis Cardinals broadcasts.

1984: Voters approve the Missouri Lottery.
06 Voters turned out in droves to pass Amendment 5, which repealed a section of the state's constitution that prohibited a lottery. There had been several earlier efforts to bring gambling to the state, but this one passed with about 70 percent of the vote. The following year, lawmakers approved Senate Bill 44, which cleared the final hurdles for the lottery to take place. Ticket sales officially began on January 20, 1986, with the instant game, "Jackpot '86." A retired butcher from Kansas City, Kansas became the Missouri Lottery's first millionaire on February 13, when he won $2.1 million.[298]

NOV 07 — 2020: Doobie Brothers are inducted into Rock and Roll Hall of Fame.

Ferguson native and lead singer for the Doobie Brothers Michael McDonald and the rest of the band were enshrined with rock and roll greats in Cleveland, Ohio. McDonald grew up in Ferguson and attended McCluer High School before setting out for music stardom. His iconic voice is heard in some of their biggest hits, including "Takin' It to the Streets," "Minute by Minute," and "What a Fool Believes," which won Song of the Year along with being on the Album of the Year in 1979. McDonald also has had a stellar solo career and has won five Grammy Awards.[299]

NOV 1967 07

An icon is born when St. Louis radio station KSHE plays "White Rabbit" by the Jefferson Airplane as the first song, following their format switch to rock 'n' roll music.

NOV 08 — 1941: O'Reilly General Hospital in Springfield is put into service.

The dedication of this Army hospital came at a pivotal time, as the United States was on the verge of entering World War II. Springfield was chosen as the site for this massive medical complex, which was designed to be a model for care. Over 100,000 patients were served during the five years O'Reilly was in operation, in the area that is now the Evangel University campus. It was closed in 1946 as an Army facility and was used as a Veterans Administration facility until 1952.[300]

NOV 1951 08

Yogi Berra wins the first of his three MVP awards.

09 1978: The McDonnell-Douglas Harrier II makes its first flight.

The revolutionary aircraft that could take off and land vertically was a showstopper, no matter where it appeared. But the AV-8B Harrier II was more than just a show piece. This tactical aircraft was one of the most impressive fighter jets ever produced, as production in St. Louis ramped up in 1981. The Harrier IIs were used in combat in Operation Desert Storm, where they were incredibly effective in just 42 days of service. Production on the line ended in 2003 after 337 aircraft were produced at a cost of around $6.5 billion.[301]

10 1907: Jane Froman is born in University City.

Froman spent much of her childhood in the small town of Clinton, but moved to Columbia just before her teen years, when she first showed an aptitude for performing. She graduated from Christian College (Columbia College), then attended Mizzou. Shortly after graduation, she began performing on the radio in Cincinnati, which led to a national appearance on NBC in 1931. From that moment on, the biggest stars of the day wanted to perform with her. She starred on the stage, on the radio, and on TV, even after sustaining severe injuries in a plane crash during a USO tour. She moved back to Columbia in her 50s and spent the rest of her life there. Her life story was immortalized in the 1952 movie, *With a Song in My Heart*.[302]

1918: World War I ends, and Missourians celebrate.

People across the state woke up to the news when whistles blew at 2:30 a.m. to announce that World War I was ending. They took to the streets later that morning to celebrate, as many cities blew their

whistles again with news of the armistice marking the cessation of hostilities at 11 in the morning—the 11th hour of the 11th day of the 11th month. Newspapers in St. Louis, Kansas City, and Springfield reported that many streets were packed with revelers who stayed for hours to celebrate the news with their neighbors.

NOV 1972 11

The new Kansas City International Airport opens with its revolutionary design. KCI garnered worldwide attention when it opened its new location north of downtown. A new feature called "Drive to Your Gate" allowed flyers to park right next to the airport terminal. The unique design had to be changed following the September 11 terror attacks. There are plans for another expansion in 2023 after voters approved a new terminal design in 2017.[303]

NOV 12 — 1998: The red carpet is rolled out for Brad Pitt.

The stars came out at the Campbell 16 Cine in Springfield as Brad Pitt held the debut of his new film, *Meet Joe Black,* in his hometown. Fans packed the red carpet at the cinema, which was only blocks away from his former stomping grounds, Kickapoo High School. The Mizzou alum also attended a $150-per-person private reception prior to the event at Twin Oaks Country Club, a short drive away.[304]

NOV 13 — 1833: The "Great Star Shower of 1833."

Many people thought the end of the world was here as a meteor shower lit up the night sky for more than four hours. There were even reports of preachers going door to door in some communities, telling residents to repent. It was actually the annual Leonid meteor shower, which hit on a mostly cloudless night over Missouri when the moon had set early, leaving a perfectly black background. Some newspapers even reported that it was bright enough that one could easily read at times during the meteor shower. [305]

NOV 14 — 1926: Paving of Route 66 between Springfield and Joplin is completed.

For several years, getting between the two cities in southwest Missouri had been unusually complicated, as there was no direct route available. Construction of the 79-mile stretch of road had taken longer than expected, and motorists were relieved to hear that it was finally completed. But Route 66 was still a patchwork of pavement, gravel, and dirt roads across the state. After the completion of this stretch of road, only 100 miles were left to be paved of the 270 miles between St. Louis and Joplin.[306]

15 1885: Phog Allen, "America's First Basketball Coach," is born in Jamesport.

Forest Clare "Phog" Allen grew up in Independence and made a name for himself as an athlete at the University of Kansas, where his coach was the legendary James Naismith, the man who invented basketball. After graduation, Allen came back to Missouri to coach at William Chrisman High School (Independence High) and eventually Warrensburg Teachers College. He then took the head coaching job at Kansas and became an icon. He coached the Jayhawks for the next 37 years, helped basketball become an Olympic sport, and coached many of the early stars we know today. Allen Fieldhouse on the campus of the University of Kansas is named in his honor.[307]

16 1826: Missouri statesman John B. Henderson is born.

The name of John Brooks Henderson may not be widely known these days, but his impact on the country was immeasurable. His family moved to Lincoln County when he was a child, and he was self-taught in nearly every subject while living on the farm—even law. He was elected to the Missouri House of Representatives in 1848 and appointed to the United States Senate in 1862. As a senator, he co-authored the 13th Amendment, which outlawed slavery and was signed by President Abraham Lincoln. Senator Henderson made history again during the presidency of Ulysses S. Grant when Grant appointed him to prosecute the Whiskey Ring case in St. Louis, making Henderson the first recognized special prosecutor in American history.[308]

NOV 1818 16

Saint Louis University is founded as the oldest college west of the Mississippi.

17 1786: Birthday of Dr. Benoist Troost, an early Kansas City leader.

Thousands of people drive Troost Avenue or enjoy Troost Park in Kansas City every day, yet few may know about their namesake. Dr. Troost was born in Holland but arrived in Missouri as Kansas City's first physician, although there appears to be some uncertainty about his medical degrees and training. Regardless, he arrived around the time the city was incorporated and became one of the city's first trustees. He was also behind the first newspaper in the city, the *Kansas City Enterprise*.[309]

18 1928: The debut of Mickey Mouse.

Walt Disney was quoted as saying, "I only hope that we never lose sight of one thing—that it was all started by a mouse." He was talking, of course, about Mickey Mouse, who made his debut in Disney's first sound-synchronized animated film, *Steamboat Willie*. Disney's impact on generations of children is impossible to measure, and his career started in Missouri. Disney and his family moved to Marceline in 1906 when he was four. As an adult, he told Marceline residents during a visit in 1956, "My best memories are the years I spent here. You children are lucky to live here." Disney also lived in Kansas City, where he first began Laugh-O-Gram films in 1922.[310]

Walt Disney, courtesy of the Library of Congress

NOV 19 | 1981: Rolling Stones' *Tattoo You* tour hits the Checkerdome.

The record-breaking concert tour almost didn't happen because singer Mick Jagger said he was tired of touring. Had it not been for the "nagging" of other band members, he likely would not have relented. The tour came to St. Louis, where the band played in front of 18,700 raucous fans at the old Checkerdome. About a month later, on December 14 and 15, the band played in front of crowds of 35,000 at the Kemper Arena in Kansas City.[311]

NOV 1989 19

NASCAR driver Rusty Wallace of Arnold wins the Winston Cup Series Championship.

NOV 20 | 1983: The made-for-tv drama, *The Day After*, captivates audiences while showing the fictional destruction of Kansas City.

An estimated 100 million viewers tuned in to see the controversial movie based on the continuing friction between the United States and Russia. The Cold War was in full swing as filmmakers gave audiences a look at what life might look like if both countries continued down the road toward nuclear war. The film drew on the fact that numerous missile silos were stationed in western Missouri, so Kansas City was an obvious target of the Soviet Union. President Ronald Reagan was given a preview of the film and he said it left him depressed.[312]

NOV 2002 20

The Bachelor season finale on ABC is watched by practically everyone in Springfield, as Aaron Buerge picks Helene Eksterowicz on national TV.

21 1980: Who Shot J. R.?

One of the most-watched TV moments in history takes place as 53 million Americans tune into CBS TV to watch *Dallas*. As with most major television programs, *Dallas* did have Missouri connections. The patriarch of the Ewing clan was Jock Ewing, played by Jim Davis. Davis was a legendary TV star who grew up in Edgerton in Platte County. He was diagnosed with cancer during his years playing Jock Ewing, and died during season five of the show. Even after his death, his beloved character was remembered, with his portrait often appearing in the background on the set.[313]

22 1944: *Meet Me in St. Louis* makes its world debut.

One of the biggest feature films to showcase St. Louis was released by Metro-Goldwyn-Mayer. *Meet Me in St. Louis* starred Judy Garland and was set in St. Louis in the year before the 1904 World's Fair. The movie had its big-screen premiere in St. Louis on November 22, 1944, then opened in New York City on November 28 before going nationwide in 1945. The film was nominated for four Oscars and won numerous major theatrical awards.[314]

23 1871: The Missouri School of Mines and Metallurgy opens in Rolla.

One of the first universities in the country to specialize in technology and engineering opened in south-central Missouri, thanks in large part to the Morrill Act of 1862. The college was designed around sciences, especially mining, due to the large industrial needs in Missouri at the time. The institution changed its name to reflect that role as the University of Missouri-Rolla, or UMR, in 1964. The school changed names again in 2008 to Missouri University of Science and Technology to showcase its top-tier ranking once again as a technological institution that has produced many NASA astronauts, brilliant nuclear scientists, physicists, and computer scientists.[315]

NOV 24 — 2007: Mizzou defeats Kansas.

Mizzou beats undefeated Kansas 36-28 at Arrowhead Stadium, elevating the Tigers to the No. 1 ranking in the polls. Chase Daniel threw 361 yards for the win.

2007 Border War at Arrowhead Stadium

NOV 25 — 1911: First homecoming game in history is held at Mizzou.

It has been a source of debate for years, but history shows that the first homecoming game in history was played between the University of Missouri and the University of Kansas in Columbia. The historic game was the idea of Missouri Athletic Director Chester Brewer, who wanted the entire university to put forth the effort to encourage alumni to come home to campus, to inaugurate the location of the new football field and reinvigorate the program. His idea was a success, drawing an estimated 10,000 fans to the game, which ended in a 3–3 tie.[316]

NOV 1935 25

A public hearing took place in the city of St. Louis on a proposal to ban car radios.

Auto parade at 1904 World's Fair

NOV 26 1904: President Theodore Roosevelt comes to St. Louis for the World's Fair.

Several dignitaries visited the fair, none more prominent than President Teddy Roosevelt. He waited until after he won the 1904 election to visit the fair, in order to avoid being accused of using the fair as a platform for his reelection. During his time at the fair, Roosevelt met with Geronimo, who was still a prisoner of war at the time, although not locked up. A few months later Geronimo rode in the president's inaugural parade, despite some calling him "the greatest single-handed murderer in American history." Will Rogers also gave a performance for President Roosevelt during the visit to the fair.[317]

NOV 1939 26
Singer Tina Turner is born in Tennessee; she would move to St. Louis as a child.

NOV 27 — 1890: The University of Missouri–Columbia plays its first football game against another school, Washington University in St. Louis.

The Mizzou Tigers are the most high-profile football program in the state, but they certainly aren't the oldest. The Washington University Bears had already been playing football for three years before the Tigers organized a team and scheduled a game. The teams met for the first time on Thanksgiving Day in St. Louis in front of 3,000 fans. Washington University won that first match 28-0.[318]

NOV 28 — 1959: Saint Louis University wins the first-ever NCAA Division I Men's Soccer Championship.

It's one thing to win a national title; it is another thing to win the inaugural one. That's exactly what the SLU Billikens soccer team did in 1959, when the team defeated the University of Bridgeport 5-2, finishing the season 11-1. Over the first 15 years of

NCAA soccer, Saint Louis University won 10 national championships, including 1959, 1960, 1962, 1963, 1965, 1967, 1969, 1970, 1972, and 1973, which is still unprecedented. More than 100 alumni have gone on to play professionally.[319]

NOV 29 — 1988: A massive fire in Kansas City claims the lives of six firefighters.

The fire broke out early in the morning in south Kansas City at a highway construction site. Firefighters rushed to the scene, where two separate fires were burning. About 30 minutes after crews arrived, a trailer containing about 25,000 pounds of ammonium nitrate and fuel oil exploded, killing six firefighters who were assigned to two separate pumpers. Five people were later convicted of starting the fires, although later investigations put those convictions in question.[320]

NOV 1922 29

The cornerstone for the Memorial Union Tower is set at the University of Missouri–Columbia.

NOV 30 — 1843: The first Thanksgiving to be observed in the state of Missouri is held.

The annual celebration began following a proclamation by Governor Thomas Reynolds. The date was later established as the fourth Thursday in November in 1877, but at the time it was celebrated on the last Thursday of the month. It wasn't until 1855, though, that the date was made an official business holiday.

NOV 1835 30

Writer Samuel L. Clemens (Mark Twain) is born in Florida, Missouri.

DECEMBER

DEC 01 1999: Sign vandalism in Missouri makes national headlines, as the KKK Adopt-a-Highway sign is stolen for a second time.

When the Ku Klux Klan sponsored the cleanup of a portion of Interstate 55 south of St. Louis, it became a hot-button issue in Jefferson City as lawmakers debated whether the organization should be allowed to participate. A US District Court

DEC 1904 01 The World's Fair comes to a close as David Francis says, "Farewell to all thy splendor."

judge decided that the group had the right to adopt the stretch of road, and the signs went up. They didn't last long, though as they were stolen nearly as quickly as they were erected. The legislature did act, however, and renamed the stretch of highway the "Rosa Parks Highway." Klan members never did clean up the highway and were eventually removed from the sponsorship program. [321]

DEC 02 1897: Voters approve a measure for Westport to be annexed by Kansas City.

At one point in Missouri's history, Westport and Kansas City were two different cities. Westport was a prosperous little town and one of the last points where westward travelers could get supplies before they left "civilization." However, Kansas City became the larger and more influential town after the Civil War. Once voters approved the annexation, the merger was finalized in 1899 in a ruling by the Missouri Supreme Court.[322]

DEC 03 — 1990: All eyes are on Missouri as a major earthquake is predicted.

Missourians had been stocking up on necessities for weeks after scientist Iben Browning predicted a major earthquake could hit on this day. His research led him to believe there was a 50 percent chance that the New Madrid seismic fault zone would become active and give the area a jolt like what was experienced in 1811. All day long, people from the Bootheel and across the Midwest were anxiously waiting to see if the ground would move. The event did help raise awareness of the fault dangers, but nothing happened.[323]

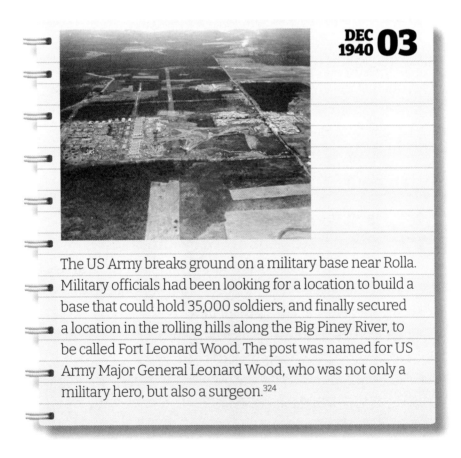

DEC 1940 03

The US Army breaks ground on a military base near Rolla. Military officials had been looking for a location to build a base that could hold 35,000 soldiers, and finally secured a location in the rolling hills along the Big Piney River, to be called Fort Leonard Wood. The post was named for US Army Major General Leonard Wood, who was not only a military hero, but also a surgeon.[324]

DEC 04

2009: *Up in the Air* with George Clooney hits the big screen, with St. Louis as the backdrop.

For several weeks in early 2009, the only thing that people in St. Louis were talking about was where George Clooney was spotted that day. Much of the movie was shot in the area, and hundreds of locals were cast as extras. So when the movie debuted, it seemed almost everyone in the city packed the movie theaters to see what neighborhoods and neighbors were included in the final edits. The movie was a massive hit, grossing nearly $170 million worldwide at the box office and receiving six Oscar nominations, including for "Best Picture."[325]

DEC 05

1994: The International Arms Reduction Treaty goes into force.

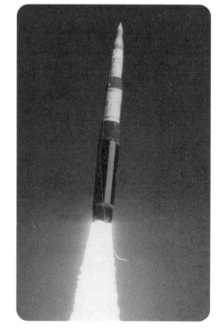

Minuteman missile silos across the state of Missouri were decommissioned after the treaty, signed in 1991, between the United States and Russia went into effect. It was surprising to many people that the state was the home to 165 Minuteman II missile sites. These were underground, fully operational, high-alert facilities spread across 14 counties in middle and western Missouri. They contained missiles capable of flying nearly 8,000 miles with incredible precision and power. The only remaining Minuteman II control center, at Whiteman AFB in Knob Noster, is open to visitors.[326]

DEC 06 1875: Albert Bond Lambert is born.

Few people have had an impact on the state of Missouri quite like Lambert. He grew up in a wealthy family—his father had founded Lambert Pharmaceuticals, makers of Listerine. Great wealth allowed him to make connections with influential people like Orville Wright, who gave Lambert his first airplane ride. His love of flying allowed him to develop a flying center west of the city, which later became Lambert Airport. There, he became friends with Charles Lindbergh and helped him in make aviation history with the famous *Spirit of St. Louis* flight.[327]

DEC 2001 06

Isle of Capri Casino opens in Boonville.

DEC 07 1941: Attack on Pearl Harbor, "A date which will live in infamy."

Those were the words used by President Franklin Roosevelt after American forces were bombed by Japan. Some 2,390 American service members and civilians died in the attack, including dozens of Missourians. In the aftermath, George Whiteman of Sedalia was the first American airman killed in World War II, when his plane was hit by Japanese pilots as he took off to battle the invasion. Whiteman Air Force Base is named in his honor.

George Whiteman

DEC 08 — 1991: *60 Minutes* puts Branson in the national spotlight.

Branson got national attention after CBS News aired a profile about the city called "The Sound of Music." The program profiled the small town in the Missouri Ozark Mountains and explained to Americans why the area is so popular with tourists. When the program aired, the population of Branson was around 4,000, and by 2020 it was at 11,567, with an estimated 7.2 million tourists visiting the town annually. The growth cannot be tied directly to that program, but when millions of viewers around the country were told that Branson was the "live music capital of the entire universe," it certainly didn't hurt.[328]

DEC 09 — 1878: Joseph Pulitzer buys the *St. Louis Dispatch* for $2,500.

Pulitzer arrived in the city penniless as a teen, and he took jobs such as waiter and reporter. His intellect got the attention of powerful people in the city, though, and he found himself in politics, even winning a spot in the state legislature at age 22. After becoming disillusioned with politics, all before the age of 30, Pulitzer bought the newspaper at a sheriff's sale, then immediately merged it with the *St. Louis Post*, to create the *Post-Dispatch*. His endowment to Columbia University led to

Joseph Pulitzer

the establishment in 1917 of the Pulitzer Prizes, which recognize the best in American journalism.[329]

1980 The first Braggin' Rights basketball game is held in St. Louis between the Mizzou Tigers and the University of Illinois Fighting Illini.

Although the teams have a rivalry dating back to 1932, things escalated a notch when the annual matchup between the two squads moved to a neutral site midway between the two campuses. The games were first played at the old St. Louis Arena, then later moved to the Enterprise Center.[330]

DEC
1884 **10**

Mark Twain's classic, *The Adventures of Huckleberry Finn*, is published.

1933: The Nelson-Atkins Museum of Art opens in Kansas City.

The Nelson-Atkins Museum of Art, recognized for the iconic badminton shuttlecocks on the lawn, helped put the Kansas City arts scene on the international map when it opened. The name of the museum comes from a pair of wealthy families who helped make sure Kansas Citians had access to the arts. The land where the museum sits is the former home of William Rockhill Nelson, called Oak Hall. Nelson was the former publisher of the *Kansas City Star* who dictated in his will that proceeds from his estate would go to purchase art for public enjoyment. Mary McAfee Atkins was a schoolteacher who was

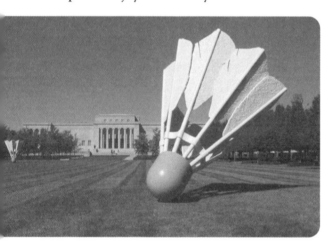

married to a wealthy real estate investor, and she also left her estate to be used for similar purposes. Today, the Nelson-Atkins Museum holds nearly 40,000 works of art from all over the world, representing all genres of art.[331]

DEC 1997 **11**

Grant Wistrom wins the Lombardi Award as the nation's top collegiate lineman. The Webb City native played college football at Nebraska before being drafted sixth overall by the St. Louis Rams. He won two state championships in high school, three national titles as a Cornhusker, and a Super Bowl with the Rams.

DEC 12 | ## 1938: The Supreme Court rules in the *Gaines v. Canada* racial discrimination case.

"Separate but equal" laws took a major blow as the United States' highest court ruled that Black student Lloyd Gaines should be admitted to the University of Missouri School of Law, because the state did not have an equal college for Black law students. The university offered to pay for Gaines to attend a law school in another state that had no admissions restrictions based on race, and Gaines refused and sued. The justices also ruled that the state had the option of establishing a law school solely for Black students, which the state did by establishing the Lincoln University School of Law in St. Louis in 1939. However, prior to his admission, Gaines disappeared and was never seen again. He was later awarded a posthumous law degree from Mizzou, and his portrait hangs in the law school.[332]

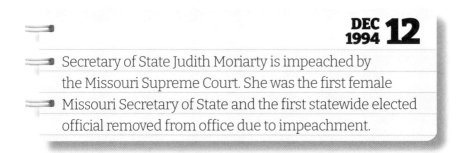

DEC 1994 12

Secretary of State Judith Moriarty is impeached by the Missouri Supreme Court. She was the first female Missouri Secretary of State and the first statewide elected official removed from office due to impeachment.

DEC 13 | ## 1987: St. Louis Cardinals football team plays its final game in St. Louis.

The Cardinals professional football team came to St. Louis in 1960 after 62 years in Chicago. They originally played at Sportsman's Park but moved into Busch Memorial Stadium in 1966, along with their baseball counterparts. The "Big Red" called Missouri their home for 27 years before moving to Tempe, Arizona in 1987. During their tenure in St. Louis, the team won the National Football Conference - Eastern Division in 1974 and 1975, but only made the playoffs a total of three years.[333]

2005: The Taum Sauk Reservoir fails, sending 1.3 billion gallons of water down the mountain.

The reservoir on top of Proffit Mountain near Lesterville was a tourist attraction, due to the unique feature of a massive body of water on the top of mountain. That feature led to disaster when one side gave way and a flash flood took out everything in its path. The wall of water was reportedly 20 feet high, rushing toward the Black River below. Giant trees were uprooted, and massive boulders were carried downstream. It took several years for a new dam and power plant to be completed and for Johnson's Shut-Ins State Park to be opened to the public once again.[334]

1965: The *Gemini 6A* blasts off from Cape Kennedy in Florida.

Walter Schirra and Thomas Stafford were the astronauts on board the spacecraft, which had been manufactured in St. Louis at McDonnell Aircraft Corporation. McDonnell had won the contract to build the space vehicles, making St. Louis ground zero for America's human spaceflight program. The *Gemini* vehicles were based off the *Mercury* spacecraft but were modified to hold two NASA astronauts. McDonnell also built the 20 *Mercury* space capsules, including Freedom 7, which was the craft piloted by Alan Shepard in America's first human spaceflight.[335]

1811: The first shocks of the New Madrid earthquake are felt.

The strongest earthquake in American history began on this date, with aftershocks rocking the Bootheel and much of the Midwest for days. The shocks were so strong that the Mississippi River even flowed backward, and Reelfoot Lake was formed when the course of the river was changed. Church bells in Philadelphia even rang, as the quake sent tremors pulsing across the country. The series of shocks took place from 1811 to 1812 and had a footprint about 10 times larger than that of the 1906 San Francisco earthquake. The one blessing was the area was sparsely populated at the time, so there were very few injuries.[336]

DEC 17 | 1993: The first B-2 Stealth Bomber touches down at Whiteman Air Force Base.

Knob Noster became the home of one of the most technologically advanced aircraft ever produced. The B-2s were part of a top-secret government project to develop aircraft that would be invisible to radar. Many people initially thought the jets would have to be extremely small to evade detection, so there was a great deal of surprise when the massive jets were finally unveiled. They were big enough to carry nuclear weapons and could fly across the globe undetected. Congressman Ike Skelton made the announcement on January 5, 1987 that the base in mid-Missouri near Sedalia would be home to the stealth aircraft, giving the region an economic and civic boost.[337]

DEC 2018 17

A hunter from Barton County is sentenced to watch Disney's *Bambi* repeatedly during his year-long prison sentence, after being convicted of killing hundreds of deer illegally.

DEC 18 | 1877: Long-distance telephone service begins in Missouri.

The very first long-distance phone call was made by Alexander Graham Bell on August 10, 1876, between the cities of Brantford and Paris in Ontario, Canada. It was only a six-mile call, and it was only one way. Two-way communications came in October of that year. But that technological advance set the stage for rapid growth of the telephone system across the US. Sixteen months after that first call, the first lines were run between Jackson and Cape Girardeau, connecting the cities via phone service in southeast Missouri. Weeks after that, St. Louis and Hannibal, then Columbia and Rocheport, were also connected.[338]

DEC 19 — 1984: Callaway Nuclear Power Plant goes into operation.

Missouri's first and only nuclear power plant had been debated for years before ground was broken in September of 1975. Even after the facility got the necessary approval following the federal government's evaluation process, it was nearly a decade before it began operating near Fulton in Callaway County. The first nuclear chain reaction happened in October of 1984, and in two months it was fully operational. The giant cooling tower can be seen for miles on a clear day in mid-Missouri, and the nuclear power plant is expected to generate electricity through at least 2044.[339]

DEC 20 — 1820: Missouri imposes a $1 bachelor tax.

One year before Missouri officially became the 24th state, our state legislators came up with an idea to help encourage marriage and boost our population via a higher birthrate. The lawmakers passed the $1 annual tax on unmarried men between the ages of 21 and 50. If you remained unmarried the entire time, your total tax bill would reach up to $30. One dollar was a modest sum even in the early 1800s and would only equal about $20 today, and there are few records to show how often the tax was collected.[340]

DEC 21 **1949: The city of Creve Coeur is incorporated.**

The beautiful St. Louis suburb got its melancholy name from a legend that has been told in the area for decades. Creve Coeur means "broken heart" in French, and the legend is that a Native American girl named Me-Me-Ton-Wish jumped from the bluffs west of the town after her heart was broken by a French-Canadian trapper. The name could also have come from the shape of Creve Coeur Lake, which may have resembled a broken heart early in the area's history. [341]

DEC 1847 21

The first telegraph message to reach Missouri was sent to the *Missouri Republican* newspaper in St. Louis from Louisville.

DEC 22 **1945: The busiest day in the history of St. Louis Union Station.**

Train stations across the country were packed with soldiers returning home from World War II. On busy days, more than 100,000 travelers would make their way through Union Station, but this day was especially busy, as travelers reported lines of people at every door and hardly any floor space available for standing. The increase in traffic came due to homecomings and celebrations taking place across the state, as soldiers and civilians packed railcars and automobiles to head home following one of the most perilous times in US history.[342]

DEC 23 — 1929: Bowling legend Dick Weber is born.

Weber moved to Florissant in 1955, when St. Louis was the epicenter of bowling competitions, and he joined the famous Budweiser bowling team. Along with Don Carter, Weber was a star in a city of sports stars in the late '50s and early '60s. He won Bowler of the Year honors in 1961, 1963, and 1965, while also racking up 26 Pro Bowling Association tournament titles, as bowling also became a widely watched spectator sport in person and on television. He was a star on the circuit for decades, becoming the first bowler to win a title in six different decades.[343]

DEC 1965 23 Busch Stadium II is "topped out" as baseball fans come to celebrate the event, just days before Christmas.

DEC 24 — 1988: Shell Oil pipeline ruptures under the Gasconade River.

The day before Christmas, people near Vienna and further downstream watched their river turn black. The 22-inch pipeline that ran between Wood River, Illinois, and Oklahoma ruptured about 20 miles north of Rolla, sending 860,000 gallons of crude oil into the pristine river in what was the worst inland oil spill in US history. The spill was made worse because it happened in such a remote part of Missouri that company officials didn't realize what had happened. The oil eventually found its way to the Mississippi River, where it affected water treatment plants and led to workers at companies like Anheuser-Busch being laid off because the water had an oily smell. The spill was largely forgotten by most people because, exactly three months later, on March 24, 1989, the *Exxon Valdez* tanker crashed in Alaska, causing an even larger environmental disaster.[344]

DEC 25 **1925: A string of lights at Country Club Plaza is lit, paving the way for a Christmas tradition that continues today.**

One of the most magical places in Missouri is Country Club Plaza in Kansas City at Christmas. The annual tradition brings thousands of people to the shopping center in the weeks leading up to the holiday. But it started small, with just a strand of lights over the doorway of the Mill Creek Building and a few random Christmas trees. At the time, the shopping center was still a new development by Jesse Clyde Nichols. It was struggling to find its footing because it was situated in such a remote part of the city, about five miles south of downtown. The nation's first suburban shopping center was even called "Nichols's folly," as most thought it would fail miserably. After that first year and the relative success it had, the maintenance supervisor began hanging more lights in the following years. And the rest, as they say, is history. Today, Christmas in Kansas City would not be complete without a trip to the Plaza to see the lights, and the Plaza has become one of the hottest shopping and residential areas in Missouri.[345]

DEC 26

1990: Nancy Cruzan dies after her feeding tube is removed.

A tragic story from southwest Missouri was front-page news for months as the debate over the right to die played out in front of the nation. Cruzan was a 25-year-old southwest Missouri woman who was thrown from her car in a crash in Carthage in 1983. She sustained severe injuries, including brain damage, that left her in a permanent vegetative state. She was transferred to a rehabilitation facility in Mt. Vernon, where her family fought in court to have her feeding tube removed so she could die, but the case dragged through the courts for years. Nearly eight years after the crash, legal rulings allowed the family to remove her from life support, and she died 12 days later at age 33. The case became a groundbreaking right-to-die case that was the first to be heard by the US Supreme Court.[346]

DEC 27

1915: William Howard Masters is born and eventually became a household name, along with Virginia Johnson.

Masters and Johnson became famous for their groundbreaking work in sexuality at Washington University. The 1966 book based on their research, *Human Sexual Response,* became a bestseller, although it was never intended for the masses. The book was written for medical professionals and fellow researchers, but found a wider audience during the sexual revolution, as curious readers devoured the research the couple performed on the human sexual responses of 382 women and 312 men. The Showtime series, *Masters of Sex*, was based on their lives.[347]

DEC 28

1982: Arthur Bryant dies at age 80, working at the restaurant he made famous until the end.

Bryant wasn't from Kansas City, but he certainly helped make Kansas City barbecue famous. Bryant opened his restaurant at 18th and Brooklyn, near where the Kansas City Blues, Athletics, and Chiefs once played their games. That location, and his famous ribs recipe, made him a legend. His success attracted three US presidents: Truman, Carter, and Obama. Even though Bryant is gone, the legacy lives on as Kansas City is still one of the top-ranked cities in the country when it comes to barbecue.[348]

DEC 29

1981: Clarence Cannon Dam and Mark Twain Lake are officially named.

It took an act of Congress, but the new dam in northeast Missouri was finally given a name. The process of damming the Salt River had been decades in the making, dating all the way back to the Flood Control Act of 1938. Damming the river served three purposes: controlling flooding, generating electricity, and creating a recreational hub. Mark Twain was born in the small town of Florida, Missouri, which now sits on the bank of the lake bearing his name. Clarence Cannon was a congressman from that region who helped make the project possible by supporting the Flood Control Act of 1962.[349]

DEC 1902 29

Scott Joplin's "The Entertainer" is copyrighted. It has been ranked as one of the top 10 songs of the 1900s.

189

DEC 30 · 1949: Announcement of the construction of the Southtown Famous-Barr.

The May Company announced the massive, three-story department store was being built at the corner of Chippewa Street and Kingshighway Boulevard in south St. Louis to the delight of residents. This was the only the second Famous-Barr store built outside of downtown St. Louis. When the grand opening celebration was held on August 24, 1951, an estimated 15,000 people showed up to celebrate. The store remained a shopping destination until 1992, when it closed due to competition from suburban shopping malls.[350]

DEC 31 · 1821: Governor Alexander McNair signs the bill designating the site for the "City of Jefferson."

In 1821, there were just a few buildings and scattered families living along the banks of the Missouri River in mid-Missouri. Yet early state founders picked that place as the site where state government operations would be based. They wanted it away from St. Louis, which was the territorial capital of the Louisiana Purchase area, and agreed that it needed to be central to the state. So they chose the area and gave it the name "City of Jefferson," in honor of Thomas Jefferson. The name was eventually changed to Jefferson City.

The city was laid out by Daniel Morgan Boone, the son of Daniel Boone, along the Missouri River. There were other transportation routes already existing, so roads could easily be built, and rails would soon follow. Construction on the first capitol building began in 1823 and was completed in 1826, when government operations were transferred from St. Charles to Jefferson City. Missouri holds the distinction of being the oldest state in the country to have created a city solely to serve as the seat of government.[351]

Endnotes

1. Pokin, Steve. "Pokin around: Ozarks History with Rogersville History Teachers," October 16, 2019. https://www.news-leader.com/story/news/local/ozarks/2019/10/16/young-brothers-massacre-baby-keet-death-history/3973790002/.

2. Caldwell, Bill. "The Young Brothers Massacre." Joplin Globe, July 11, 2020. https://www.joplinglobe.com/news/local_news/bill-caldwell-the-young-brothers-massacre/article_12b8925a-acfe-5a18-a53c-b853108262a9.html.

3. Hayes, Troy. "Missouri/Iowa Line Boundary Investigation." The American Surveyor, 2006. https://www.theamericansurveyor.com/PDF/TheAmericanSurveyor_MO-IABoundaryLineInvestigation_Mar-Apr2006.pdf.

4. *State of Missouri v. State of Iowa*. Accessed January 13, 2021. https://www.law.cornell.edu/supremecourt/text/165/118.

5. Morgan, Sonya. "The Original Uncle Sam Is Laid to Rest in Excelsior Springs." The Idle Hour. Morgan Sites. Accessed January 13, 2021. http://theidlehour.com/unclesam.html.

6. Holcombe, R.I. "History of Greene County, Missouri 1883." History of Greene County, Missouri. Springfield Greene County Library, September 21, 2020. https://thelibrary.org/lochist/history/holcombe/grch29pt1.html.

7. "Marlin Perkins." Saint Louis Zoo. Saint Louis Zoo, November 26, 2020. https://www.stlzoo.org/about/history/marlinperkins.

8. "Gem Stores, Inc. v. O'Brien." Justia Law. Justia Law, September 21, 2020. https://law.justia.com/cases/missouri/supreme-court/1963/50355-0.html.

9. "A St. Louis History: People." Mound City on the Mississippi. Historic Preservation, St. Louis, December 5, 2020. https://dynamic.stlouis-mo.gov/history/peopledetail.cfm?Master_ID=1961.

10. "Ralston Purina Company." Encyclopedia Britannica. Encyclopedia Britannica, inc. Accessed January 2, 2021. https://www.britannica.com/topic/Ralston-Purina-Company.

11. "The Legend of How Alumni and Locals Saw to It That the Columns Became Mizzou's Foremost Campus Icon:" Mizzou Alumni Association. Curators of the University of Missouri, October 16, 2020. https://www.mizzou.com/s/1002/alumni/19/interior.aspx?sid=1002&gid=1001&pgid=252&cid=1202&ecid=1202&crid=0&calpgid=396&calcid=960.

12. Chase, Nan. "Home Grown: Once Swallowed Whole by TWA, Local Missouri Favorite Ozark Air Lines Flies Again." *Air & Space Magazine*, January 2001. https://www.airspacemag.com/flight-today/home-grown-1796318/.

13. Missouri Secretary of State—IT. "State Symbols of Missouri." Missouri State Seal. Missouri Secretary of State. Accessed October 14, 2020. https://www.sos.mo.gov/symbol/seal.

14. Carey, Susan. "FAA Investigating Southwest Plane's Landing at Wrong Missouri Airport." The Wall Street Journal. Dow Jones & Company, January 14, 2014. https://www.wsj.com/articles/SB10001424052702304049704579318531610772954.

15. "Warren Eastman Hearnes (1923-2009)." Missouri House of Representatives. State of Missouri, November 30, 2020. https://house.mo.gov/FamousInductee.aspx?id=65#:~:text=Warren%20Eastman%20Hearnes%2C%20Missouri's%2046th,three%20branches%20of%20state%20government.

16. Malone, Ross. "January 14, 1868." *Missouri Life Magazine*, January 13, 2020. https://missourilife.com/january-14-1868/.

17. "Packers Beat Chiefs in First Super Bowl." History.com. A&E Television Networks, November 16, 2009. https://www.history.com/this-day-in-history/packers-beat-chiefs-in-first-super-bowl#:~:text=On%20January%2015%2C%201967%2C%20the,Memorial%20Coliseum%20in%20Los%20Angeles.

18. Kiner, Deb. "It's National Beer Day!" Penn Live. Advance Local Media, April 7, 2015. https://www.pennlive.com/midstate/2015/04/its_national_beer_day_vintage.html#:~:text=The%20hitch%20continued%20on%20a,on%20April%207%2C%201933.%22.

19. Sparks, Glen. "Darrell Porter." Society for American Baseball Research, October 4, 2020. https://sabr.org/bioproj/person/darrell-porter/.

20. Spradley, Mary Jane. "History." Raytown Chamber of Commerce. Raytown Area Chamber of Commerce and Tourism. Accessed November 14, 2020. http://raytownchamber.com/history/.

21. Brown, John. "Sara Evans: Arts and Entertainment." Missouri Legends. Missouri Legends, April 4, 2011. https://missourilegends.com/artists/arts-and-entertainment/sara-evans/.

22. "History of the Governor's Mansion." The Missouri Governor's Mansion, October 22, 2020. https://mansion.mo.gov/history/#:~:text=History%20of%20the%20Governor's%20 Mansion&text=The%20Missouri%20Governor's%20Mansion%20was,of%20the%20 furnishings%2C%20was%20%2474%2C960.

23. "Traditional Music of the Ozarks." Ozark Jubilee Digitization Project. Missouri State University, March 17, 2017. https://guides.library.missouristate.edu/c.php?g=701771&p=5146416.

24. Hill, Michael. "Chuck Berry." Rock & Roll Hall of Fame. Rock Hall. Accessed January 14, 2021. https://www.rockhall.com/inductees/chuck-berry.

25. "Structures: Powell Symphony Hall." Mound City on the Mississippi. St. Louis Historic Preservation. Accessed September 1, 2020. https://dynamic.stlouis-mo.gov/history/structdetail. cfm?Master_ID=1395.

26. Fournier, Ron. "Bradley Kicks off 2000 Campaign." The Washington Post. WP Company, January 25, 1999. https://www.washingtonpost.com/wp-srv/politics/campaigns/wh2000/stories/ bradley012599.htm.

27. Brinker, Jennifer. "A Look at John Paul II's Visit to St. Louis, 20 Years Later." St. Louis Review. Archdiocese of St Louis, January 18, 2019. https://www.archstl.org/a-look-at-john-paul-iis-visit-to-st-louis-20-years-later-3524.

28. "Maps: Trail of Tears National Historic Site." National Parks Service. US Department of the Interior. Accessed January 14, 2021. https://www.nps.gov/trte/planyourvisit/maps.htm.

29. Roe, Jason. "The Worst Fire in Kansas City History: KC History." The Worst Fire in Kansas City History | KC History, Kansas City Public Library, 17 Jan. 2014, kchistory.org/week-kansas-city-history/worst-fire-kansas-city-history.

30. Lockwood, Eric. "Show Me a WWII Battleship! Missouri Christened Jan. 29, 1944." The Sextant. Office of Naval History and Heritage Command, January 29, 2015. https://usnhistory.navylive. dodlive.mil/2015/01/29/show-me-a-wwii-battleship-missouri-christened-jan-29-1944/.

31. Forrester, Wade. "January 30, 2000: The Rams Win A Thriller In Super Bowl XXXIV." On This Day in Sports. Wade Forrester Blogs, January 30, 2014. http://onthisdayinsports.blogspot. com/2014/01/january-30-2000-rams-win-thriller-in.html#:~:text=January%2030%2C%20 2014-,January%2030%2C%202000%3A%20The%20Rams%20Win%20A%20Thriller%20In%20 Super,finishes%20in%20Super%20Bowl%20history.

32. "Theatre Information." The Fabulous Fox Theatre. Accessed January 14, 2021. https://www. fabulousfox.com/theatre-info.

33. Kreps, Daniel. "Nipple Ripples: Revisiting Janet Jackson's Wardrobe Malfunction." Rolling Stone. Rolling Stone, June 25, 2018. https://www.rollingstone.com/culture/culture-news/nipple-ripples-10-years-of-fallout-from-janet-jacksons-halftime-show-122792/.

34. Associated Press, ed. "Mahomes Leads Chiefs' Rally Past 49ers in Super Bowl, 31-20." ESPN. ESPN Internet Ventures, February 3, 2020. https://www.espn.com/nfl/recap?gameId=401131047.

35. Simpson, Brent. "Bagnell Dam Facts and Figures." Bagnell Dam Facts. Michael Gillespie, 2005. http://www.lakehistory.info/damfacts.html#:~:text=Construction%20began%20on%20 August%206,the%20dam%20sluiceways%20were%20closed.

36. Karnes, Sara. "Rockaway Beach Rekindles Casino Idea." Branson Tri-Lakes News, September 23, 2016. https://www.bransontrilakesnews.com/news_free/article_7d21927c-80df-11e6-8958-6fd9fbc0c77d.html.

37. "History." Silver Dollar City Attractions. Accessed December 14, 2020. https://www. silverdollarcity.com/theme-park/Guest-Services/History.

38. "Missouri History: Missouri State Capitol." Missouri Records and Archives. Missouri Secretary of State's Office. Accessed September 11, 2020. https://www.sos.mo.gov/archives/history/capitol.

39. Bellis, Mary. "Who Invented the Microchip?" ThoughtCo. Dotdash Publishing, March 31, 2017. https://www.thoughtco.com/jack-kilby-father-of-the-microchip-1992042.

40. "Laura's Life on Rocky Ridge Farm." Laura Ingalls Wilder Historic Home & Museum, December 16, 2019. https://lauraingallswilderhome.com/lauras-life-on-rocky-ridge-farm/.

41. "Historic Kirkwood." Landmarks Walking Tour. Kirkwood Landmarks Commission, 2013. https://www.kirkwoodmo.org/home/showpublisheddocument?id=827.

42. "Thomas Reynolds, 1840-1844." Missouri State Archives and Records. Missouri Secretary of State's Office. Accessed October 22, 2020. https://www.sos.mo.gov/archives/mdh_splash/default. asp?coll=treynolds.

43. "Soulard Farmers Market." Wikipedia. Wikimedia Foundation, July 21, 2020. https://en.wikipedia.org/wiki/Soulard_Farmers_Market#cite_note-Fox_Missouri_Historical_Society_1995_p._52-1.

44. History.com Editors, ed. "Dred Scott Case." History.com. A&E Television Networks, October 27, 2009. https://www.history.com/topics/black-history/dred-scott-case.

45. Brown, John. "JC Penney: Missouri Business Legend." Missouri Legends, March 14, 2011. https://missourilegends.com/missouri-business-legends/j-c-penney/.

46. Kelly, Matt. "The Negro National League Is Founded." Baseball Hall of Fame. National Baseball Hall of Fame and Museum. Accessed November 12, 2020. https://baseballhall.org/discover-more/stories/inside-pitch/negro-national-league-is-founded#:~:text=On%20Feb.,diamond%20alongside%20their%20white%20teammates.

47. "Jamie McMurray Wins 52nd Annual Daytona 500." Daytona International Speedway, February 14, 2010. https://www.daytonainternationalspeedway.com/Articles/2010/02/Jamie-McMurray-Wins-52nd-Annual-Daytona-500.aspx.

48. BN Staff, ed. "On This Day: Leon Spinks Shocks Muhammad Ali and the World." Boxing News Kelsey Media. February 15, 2020. https://www.boxingnewsonline.net/on-this-day-leon-spinks-shocked-muhammad-ali-and-the-world/.

49. "Fulton State Hospital." Asylum Projects. Accessed September 26, 2020. http://www.asylumprojects.org/index.php?title=Fulton_State_Hospital.

50. Henson McClure, Jeanette. "History of Iron County, Missouri." Roots Web. Ancestry.com. Accessed December 20, 2020. http://sites.rootsweb.com/~moicgs/countyhistory.html.

51. "History of Pacific." Pacific, MO. City of Pacific. Accessed January 14, 2021. https://www.pacificmissouri.com/199/History.

52. "A Look Back at 40 Years of Soulard Mardi Gras Fun." STLtoday.com. *St. Louis Post-Dispatch*, April 22, 2020. https://www.stltoday.com/news/archives/a-look-back-at-40-years-of-soulard-mardi-gras-fun/collection_fbc040cf-6c3e-5174-b7e6-bc7ce6646eb8.html.

53. Associated Press. "Cardinals Take Pujols From $950K to $100M." Newsday. Newsday, June 1, 2009. https://www.newsday.com/sports/cardinals-take-pujols-from-950k-to-100m-1.703000.

54. O'Neil, Tim. "'The Greatest Funeral Pageant Ever Seen in the West' in 1891 as Gen. Sherman Was Laid to Rest in St. Louis." STLtoday.com. *St. Louis Post-Dispatch*, April 22, 2020. https://www.stltoday.com/news/archives/the-greatest-funeral-pageant-ever-seen-in-the-west-in-1891-as-gen-sherman-was/article_159e2805-93fa-5ff7-ad96-7cb0aee5ffc0.html.

55. "Founders Day." Washington University in St. Louis. Accessed January 14, 2021. https://alumni.wustl.edu/alumni/awards/founders/Pages/about-founders-day.aspx#:~:text=On%20February%2022%2C%201853%E2%80%94George,into%20law%2C%20establishing%20Eliot%20Seminary.

56. Delach Leonard, Mary. "20 Years Ago, Route 66 State Park Rose From The Ashes Of Times Beach." St. Louis Public Radio, August 28, 2019. https://news.stlpublicradio.org/government-politics-issues/2019-08-26/20-years-ago-route-66-state-park-rose-from-the-ashes-of-times-beach.

57. "Lindenwood University." Wikipedia. Wikimedia Foundation, January 11, 2021. https://en.wikipedia.org/wiki/Lindenwood_University.

58. "Whoosh! The Day the Screamin' Eagle Made Its Six Flags Debut." STLtoday.com. *St. Louis Post-Dispatch*, May 26, 2020. https://www.stltoday.com/news/archives/whoosh-the-day-the-screamin-eagle-made-its-six-flags-debut/collection_8820376c-a702-53d1-a76c-ad0693df2134.html.

59. Ressel, Teresa. "Supreme Court Ruling Leaves Conceal and Carry up in the Air, but Sheriff Says He Will Issue Permits Anyway." Daily Journal Online, February 27, 2004. https://dailyjournalonline.com/news/local/supreme-court-ruling-leaves-conceal-and-carry-up-in-the-air-but-sheriff-says-he/article_c19aca33-64a7-5193-806c-b2f04e6bd407.html.

60. Hunt Nassaney, Jeanne, ed. "Old Plank Road Was History Link For Farmington Area Communities." Roots Web. Ancestry.com. Accessed January 14, 2021. https://sites.rootsweb.com/~mostfran/towns/plankroad_history.htm.
Originally published in The Daily Journal, Flat River, Mo., Monday, March 19, 1979

61. "Final Episode of M*A*S*H Airs." History.com. A&E Television Networks, November 13, 2009. https://www.history.com/this-day-in-history/final-episode-of-mash-airs.

62. Regenbogen, Joe. "Racial Segregation in St. Louis." Center for the Humanities. Washington University in St. Louis, August 30, 2018. https://humanities.wustl.edu/nnr-summer-institute/425.

63. Reichhardt, Tony. "Berry's Leap." Air & Space Magazine. *Air & Space Magazine*, February 29, 2012. https://www.airspacemag.com/daily-planet/berrys-leap-111412656/#:~:text=The%20 occasion%3A%20the%20100th%20anniversary,parachute%20jump%20from%20an%20 airplane.&text=On%20March%201%2C%201912%2C%20U.S.,as%20the%20first%20airline%20 pilot.

64. Roe, Jason. "End of the Marriage Penalty: KC History." KC History. The Kansas City Public Library. Accessed January 14, 2021. https://kchistory.org/week-kansas-city-history/end-marriage-penalty.

65. "Jean Harlow." Encyclopedia Britannica. Encyclopedia Britannica, inc., June 3, 2020. https://www.britannica.com/biography/Jean-Harlow.

66. Senate Historical Office, ed. "Senate Stories: David Rice Atchison: (Not) President for a Day." United State Senate, December 14, 2020. https://www.senate.gov/artandhistory/senate-stories/no-david-rice-atchison-was-not-president-for-a-day.htm#:~:text=A%20plaque%20affixed%20 to%20a%20statue%20in%20Plattsburg%2C%20Missouri%2C%20reads,presidency%20was%20 March%204%2C%201849.

67. "The Sinews of Peace ('Iron Curtain Speech')." International Churchill Society, December 7, 2020. https://winstonchurchill.org/resources/speeches/1946-1963-elder-statesman/the-sinews-of-peace/.

68. Shedden, David. "Today in Media History: Walter Cronkite Retired as CBS Evening News Anchor in 1981." Poynter. Poynter Institute, March 5, 2015. https://www.poynter.org/reporting-editing/2015/today-in-media-history-walter-cronkite-retired-as-cbs-evening-news-anchor-in-1981/#:~:text=in%20your%20browser.-,March%206%2C%201981,that's%20the%20way%20it%20 is%E2%80%A6%E2%80%9D.

69. Smith, Alex. "COVID-19 Was In Missouri A Month Before The First Case Was Reported, According To Updated Data." St. Louis Public Radio, December 2, 2020. https://news.stlpublicradio.org/2020-05-27/covid-19-was-in-missouri-a-month-before-the-first-case-was-reported-according-to-updated-data.

70. Franklin, Wes. "Touring the Missouri State Pen." Neosho Daily News, August 18, 2020. https://www.neoshodailynews.com/news/20200818/touring-missouri-state-pen.

71. Brown, John. "Ella Ewing: Historical Missourian." Missouri Legends, March 8, 2014. https://missourilegends.com/history-and-politics/ella-ewing/.

72. Beherer, Thomas. "BLUE LAW BLUDGEONED: Missouri Ends 137-Year-Old Law." Desert Sun. March 14, 1963. https://cdnc.ucr.edu/cgi-bin/cdnc?a=d&d=DS19630314.2.35&e=-------en--20-- 1--txt-txIN--------1

73. Bryant, Tim. "Workers Prepare Admiral for a Scrap Yard." STLtoday.com. *St. Louis Post-Dispatch*, May 16, 2017. https://www.stltoday.com/business/local/workers-prepare-admiral-for-a-scrap-yard/article_9f4d21c4-bdef-5f89-bf42-dab02ed60039.htm.

74. "Dick Weber Exhibit." Bowling Museum & Hall of Fame. Accessed January 14, 2021. https://www.bowlingmuseum.com/Visit/Online-Exhibits/Dick-Weber-Exhibit.

75. "Guide to African American History." Missouri Digital Heritage. Missouri Secretary of State's Office. Accessed January 14, 2021. https://www.sos.mo.gov/mdh/curriculum/africanamerican/guide/rg600.

76. Bradbury, Jr., John F. "The Early Years of Route 66 in Phelps County, Missouri." OzarksWatch. Springfield Greene County Library, 1994. https://thelibrary.org/lochist/periodicals/ozarkswatch/ow702n.htm.

77. Pierce, Todd James. "Walt Disney and Riverfront Square." Disney History Institute, February 21, 2015. https://www.disneyhistoryinstitute.com/2013/04/walt-disney-and-riverfront-square-part-8.html.

78. "The Day the Billikens Sat atop the World of College Basketball." STLtoday.com. St. Louis Post Dispatch, April 22, 2020. https://www.stltoday.com/news/archives/the-day-the-billikens-sat-atop-the-world-of-college-basketball/collection_94487b72-27c5-5fb8-a0d4-fff1588e3970.html#2.

79. "Isaac Charles Parker." Wikipedia. Wikimedia Foundation, December 30, 2020. https://en.wikipedia.org/wiki/Isaac_Charles_Parker.

80. "America's First Lager Beer Brewers." Lemp Family History. The Lemp Mansion. Accessed October 31, 2020. https://www.lempmansion.com/history.htm.

81. Tech2 Staff, ed. "Jack Dorsey Sent out the First Tweet 13 Years Ago Today." Tech2. FirstPost, March 22, 2019. https://www.firstpost.com/tech/news-analysis/jack-dorsey-sent-out-the-first-tweet-13-years-ago-today-heres-how-to-find-yours-6305921.html#:~:text=On%2021%20 March%202006%20(22,'Twttr'%20and%20not%20Twitter.

82. "The Missouri State Flag." Missouri State Archives. Missouri Secretary of State's Office. Accessed February 2, 2020. https://www.sos.mo.gov/Kids/history/flag.

83. Absher, Frank. "WEW's Roller Coaster History Began In March 1922." St. Louis Media History. St. Louis Media History Foundation. Accessed September 14, 2020. https://www.stlmediahistory.org/index.php/Radio/RadioArticles/wews-roller-coaster-history-began-in-march-1922.

84. "Stiles Scores 41, SW Missouri Upsets Duke." *The Washington Post*. WP Company, March 25, 2001. https://www.washingtonpost.com/archive/sports/2001/03/25/stiles-scores-41-sw-missouri-upsets-duke/e2405b00-76cc-47ba-9161-e78ef41d3dc6/.

85. "1934: Horton Smith Wins the Inaugural Masters at Augusta National." Golf History Today, March 26, 2019. https://golfhistorytoday.com/1934-horton-smith-inaugural-master/.

86. Brown, John. "Missouri Legends: Tennessee Williams." Missouri Legends, June 14, 2011. https://missourilegends.com/artists/arts-and-entertainment/tennessee-williams/

87. Klein, Mike. "Webster University Wins 5th Straight President's Cup." Chess.com. Chess.com, March 28, 2017. https://www.chess.com/news/view/webster-university-wins-5th-straight-president-s-cup-3692.

88. "Why Is There a Kansas City in Both Kansas and Missouri?" KC History. The Kansas City Public Library. Accessed November 27, 2020. https://kchistory.org/faq/why-there-kansas-city-both-kansas-and-missouri.

89. Brown, John. "Missouri Legends: Josephine Baker." Missouri Legends, April 4, 2011. https://missourilegends.com/artists/arts-and-entertainment/josephine-baker/.

90. Millitzer, Joe. "St. Louis Zoo Wins 'Best in the US' 2017 Title." Fox 2 KTVI. Nexstar Broadcasting, March 31, 2017. https://fox2now.com/news/st-louis-zoo-wins-best-in-the-us-2017-title/.

91. "Branson, MO USA." Encyclopedia Britannica. Encyclopedia Britannica, inc., March 3, 2013. https://www.britannica.com/place/Branson.

92. "Bennie Moten Dies." The Pendergast Years: Kansas City in the Jazz Age & Great Depression. The Kansas City Public Library. Accessed October 14, 2020. https://pendergastkc.org/timeline/bennie-moten-dies.

93. Rennie, Daniel. "The Story of Robert Ford – The 'Coward' Who Assassinated Jesse James." All That's Interesting. All That's Interesting, March 15, 2018. https://allthatsinteresting.com/robert-ford.

94. "History of the Area." City of Springfield Community History. City of Springfield, MO. Accessed October 18, 2020. https://www.springfieldmo.gov/709/History.

95. Wood, Larry. "It's All in the Past—Missouri and Ozarks History: Mayme Ousley: Missouri's First Woman Mayor." The Rolla Daily News—Rolla, MO. The Rolla Daily News—Rolla, MO, February 11, 2017. https://www.therolladailynews.com/news/20170211/its-all-in-past---missouri-and-ozarks-history-mayme-ousley-missouris-first-woman-mayor.

96. Franklin, Corey, Karen Milner, and Jamie Mahler Westbrook. "Missouri State Governor Mike Parson Issues Stay at Home Order for the Period of April 6, 2020 through April 24, 2020." JD Supra. FordHarrison, April 6, 2020. https://www.jdsupra.com/legalnews/missouri-state-governor-mike-parson-71666/.

97. "Pendergast Indicted." The Pendergast Years: Kansas City in the Jazz Age & Great Depression. The Kansas City Public Library. Accessed January 14, 2021. https://pendergastkc.org/timeline/pendergast-indicted.

98. Augustyn, Adam. "Kansas City Royals." Encyclopedia Britannica. Encyclopedia Britannica, inc., March 24, 2020. https://www.britannica.com/topic/Kansas-City-Royals.

99. "The History of Missouri's State Park System." Missouri State Parks. Department of Natural Resources, August 25, 2011. https://mostateparks.com/page/59044/history-missouris-state-park-system#:~:text=On%20April%209%2C%201917%2C%20the,parks%20once%20they%20were%20acquired.

100. McConnell, Kaitlyn. "That Time McDonald County Seceded from Missouri," April 3, 2020. https://ozarksalive.com/that-time-mcdonald-county-seceded-from-missouri/.

101. Putnam, G. W. "Four Months with Charles Dickens." The Atlantic. Atlantic Media Company, November 1, 1870. https://www.theatlantic.com/magazine/archive/1870/11/four-months-with-charles-dickens/306681/.

102. Glass, Andrew. "Truman Sworn in as 33rd President, April 12, 1945." Politico, April 12, 2018. https://www.politico.com/story/2018/04/12/harry-truman-sworn-in-as-33rd-president-april-12-1945-511037.

103. "Bond Dance Hall Explosion." Unlock the Ozarks. Unlock the Ozarks by Trillium Trust. Accessed January 14, 2021. http://www.unlocktheozarks.org/local-communities/west-plains-mo/bond-dance-hall-explosion/#:~:text=The%20Dance%20Hall%20Explosion&text=On%20a%20rainy%20night%20in,town%20of%20West%20Plains%2C%20Missouri.&text=But%20at%20around%2011%3A05,twenty%2Dthree%20more%20were%20injured.

104. "Apr. 14, 1906: Horace Duncan and Fred Coker Lynched in Springfield, Missouri." A History of Racial Injustice. Equal Justice Initiative. Accessed September 22, 2019. https://calendar.eji.org/racial-injustice/apr/14#:~:text=Horace%20Duncan%20and%20Fred%20Coker%20Lynched%20in%20Springfield%2C%20Missouri,-Image%20%7C%20The%20Sedalia&text=Shortly%20before%20midnight%20on%20April,and%20lynched%20in%20Springfield%2C%20Missouri.

105. Torchia, Robert, and Catherine Southwick. "Thomas Hart Benton: American, 1889–1975." National Gallery of Art, August 17, 2018. https://www.nga.gov/collection/artist-info.953.html#:~:text=Named%20after%20his%20great%2Duncle,%2C%20DC%2C%20and%20southwest%20Missouri.

106. "Henry Smith Pritchett." Wikipedia. Wikimedia Foundation, December 29, 2019. https://en.wikipedia.org/wiki/Henry_Smith_Pritchett.

107. "Fun Facts about Fountain Day, Which Started 125 Years Ago." FOX 4 Kansas City WDAF-TV. Nexstar Broadcasting, April 12, 2017. https://fox4kc.com/mornings/fun-facts-about-fountain-day-which-started-125-years-ago/.

108. Mitchell, Kevin. "The Big One That Got Away: Blues Were Bought, the Deal Done, but Then NHL Intervened (May 17, 2008)." thestarphoenix. The Star Phoenix, April 16, 2020. https://thestarphoenix.com/sports/hockey/nhl/the-big-one-that-got-away-blues-were-bought-the-deal-done-but-then-nhl-intervened.

109. Burnes, Brian. "Age of Coronavirus: KC's Role in Winning the War on Polio." Flatland Kansas City. Public Television 19, March 31, 2020. https://www.flatlandkc.org/news-issues/age-of-coronavirus-kcs-role-in-winning-the-war-on-polio/.

110. House, Ray. "Wilson's Creek National Battlefield." Military Wiki. Wikia.org. Accessed January 14, 2021. https://military.wikia.org/wiki/Wilson%27s_Creek_National_Battlefield.

111. The Editors of Encyclopedia Britannica, ed. "James Earl Ray." Encyclopedia Britannica. Encyclopedia Britannica, inc., April 19, 2020. https://www.britannica.com/biography/James-Earl-Ray.

112. Mohon, Lee. "Hubble Space Telescope Launches – April 24, 1990." NASA. NASA, April 25, 2018. https://www.nasa.gov/centers/marshall/history/this-week-in-nasa-history-hubble-space-telescope-launches-april-24-1990.html.

113. Shouler, Ken. "Macauley Made Everything Look Easy." ESPN. ESPN Internet Ventures, September 20, 2008. https://www.espn.com/nba/news/story?page=Macauley-111109.

114. "Ulysses S. Grant (1822 – 1885)." Historic Missourians. The State Historical Society of Missouri. Accessed October 1, 2020. https://historicmissourians.shsmo.org/historicmissourians/name/g/grant/.

115. "The Great St. Louis Metropolitan Hail Storms, April 28th, 2012." National Weather Service St. Louis, April 28, 2012. https://www.weather.gov/media/lsx/Events/04_28_2012.pdf.

116. Morin, H. (1927, April 29). San Diego Plane Takes Air in New York-Paris Flight Test. *The San Diego Union*, p. 1.

117. "History." Silver Dollar City Attractions. Accessed April 26, 2020. https://www.silverdollarcity.com/theme-park/Guest-Services/History.

118. "The Camp Jackson Interpretive Sign." The Civil War Muse. Grawader Enterprises. Accessed December 26, 2020. http://www.thecivilwarmuse.com/index.php?page=camp-jackson-2.

119. "Shelley v. Kraemer, 334 U.S. 1 (1948)." Justia Law. Accessed January 3, 2021. https://supreme.justia.com/cases/federal/us/334/1/.

120. "Tornado Outbreak Sequence of May 2003." Wikipedia. Wikimedia Foundation, January 5, 2021. https://en.wikipedia.org/wiki/Tornado_outbreak_sequence_of_May_2003.

121. Loff, Sarah. "May 5, 1961, Alan Shepard in Spacesuit Before Mercury Launch." NASA. NASA, May 5, 2016. https://www.nasa.gov/image-feature/may-5-1961-alan-shepard-in-spacesuit-before-mercury-launch.

122. "Kansas City Announces Opening Date Of The Kc Streetcar." Ride KC Streetcar. City of Kansas City, February 24, 2016. https://kcstreetcar.org/kc-streetcar-opening-date/.

123. Garrison, Chad. "Wizard of Oz Munchkin, Mickey Carroll, Dead at 89." *Riverfront Times*. *Riverfront Times*, January 2, 2021. https://www.riverfronttimes.com/artsblog/2009/05/07/wizard-of-oz-munchkin-mickey-carroll-dead-at-89.

124. Farber and Associates, LLC, ed. "The St. Louis Automobile & The St. Louis Motor Car Co.," 2012. https://www.american-automobiles.com/St-Louis.html.

125. Lotzof, Kerry. "Missouri Leviathan: The Making of an American Mastodon," 2018. https://www.nhm.ac.uk/discover/the-making-of-an-american-mastodon.html.

126. "Mrs. Annie Malone, Poro Founder, Dies." *St. Louis Post-Dispatch*. May 12, 1957. p. 6B.

127. US Census Bureau Public Information Office. "Plato, Mo. Celebrates Recognition as the 2010 Census U.S. Center of Population—2010 Census—Newsroom—US Census Bureau," May 19, 2016. https://www.census.gov/newsroom/releases/archives/2010_census/cb11-cn135.html.

128. Brown, John. "Yogi Berra, Baseball Legend," 2015. https://missourilegends.com/sports-legends/sports-legends-baseball/yogi-berra/.

129. "Car Phone," October 23, 2020. https://en.wikipedia.org/wiki/Car_phone.

130. "Lewis and Clark Expedition." Encyclopedia Britannica. Encyclopedia Britannica, inc. Accessed December 2, 2020. https://www.britannica.com/event/Lewis-and-Clark-Expedition.

131. "Bellefontaine Cemetery." Bellefontaine Cemetery. Accessed November 21, 2020. https://bellefontainecemetery.org/destination/history/.

132. Roe, Jason. "Dr. Hyde and Mr. Swope." This Week in KC History. Kansas City Public Library. Accessed October 1, 2020. https://kchistory.org/week-kansas-city-history/dr-hyde-and-mr-swope.

133. "History Shines through Springfield's Shrine Mosque." Ozarks Alive. Ozarks Alive, July 28, 2019. https://ozarksalive.com/history-shines-through-springfields-shrine-mosque/.

134. O'Neil, Tim. "May 17, 1849: The Great Fire That Changed the Face of St. Louis." STLtoday.com. *St. Louis Post-Dispatch*, May 17, 2020. https://www.stltoday.com/news/local/history/may-17-1849-the-great-fire-that-changed-the-face-of-st-louis/article_ff8faca9-1ba5-5f52-9252-e8397b705240.html.

135. "Tripping the Light Fantastic...and Then Some!" This week in KC History. Kansas City Public Library. Accessed October 25, 2020. https://kchistory.org/week-kansas-city-history/tripping-light-fantasticand-then-some.

136. "Charles Lindbergh Takes off across the Atlantic in the Spirit of St. Louis." History.com. A&E Television Networks, July 21, 2010. https://www.history.com/this-day-in-history/spirit-of-st-louis-departs.

137. Greene, Nelson 'Chip.' "May 21, 1947: Jackie Robinson Makes His Dodgers Debut in St. Louis." Society for American Baseball Research. admin /wp-content/uploads/2020/02/sabr_logo.png, April 17, 2020. https://sabr.org/gamesproj/game/may-21-1947-jackie-robinson-makes-his-dodgers-debut-in-st-louis/.

138. US Department of Commerce, NOAA. "Joplin Tornado—May 22nd, 2011." National Weather Service. NOAA's National Weather Service, May 18, 2020. https://www.weather.gov/sgf/news_events_2011may22.

139. "Wainwright Building." Wikipedia. Wikimedia Foundation, December 9, 2020. https://en.wikipedia.org/wiki/Wainwright_Building.

140. Comita, Jenny. "Jane Goodall, Karlie Kloss, and the Women of the Diane Von Furstenberg Award Are Carrying the Torch For Freedom." *W Magazine* | Women's Fashion & Celebrity News, May 24, 2017. https://www.wmagazine.com/story/diane-von-furstenberg-award-winners-women-jane-goodall-karlie-kloss/.

141. Kardell, Shelby. "Glen Echo Country Club Is a Historical Gem for St. Louis." STLtoday.com. *St. Louis Post-Dispatch*, September 11, 2016. https://www.stltoday.com/news/local/metro/glen-echo-country-club-is-a-historical-gem-for-st-louis/article_7184d9ba-2a95-59c6-913b-f9197568e47f.html.

142. "Grand Opening 1973: 10 Fun Facts." Worlds of Fun. Cedar Fair Entertainment, May 25, 2018. https://www.worldsoffun.com/blog/2018/worlds-of-fun-history-grand-opening.

143. Brown, John. "Vincent Price, Missouri Legend." Missouri Legends, January 2014. https://missourilegends.com/artists/arts-and-entertainment/vincent-price/.

144. Dyer, Robert. "A Brief History Of Steamboating On The Missouri River." Riverboat Daves, June 2, 1997. http://www.riverboatdaves.com/docs/moboats.html.

145. "MCC History—More than a Tradition." Metropolitan Community College. Accessed November 26, 2020. https://mcckc.edu/our-history/.

146. Jefferson, Brandie. "Alum Astronaut Makes History: The Source: Washington University in St. Louis." The Source. Washington University, December 4, 2020. https://source.wustl.edu/2020/06/alum-astronaut-makes-history/.

147. "The Missouri Mule." St. Louis Mercantile Library at the University of Missouri–St. Louis. Accessed January 2, 2021. https://www.umsl.edu/mercantile/events-and-exhibitions/online-exhibits/missouri-splendor/Missouri_Mule.pdf.

148. "Eric Greitens." National Governors Association. Accessed November 14, 2020. https://www.nga.org/governor/eric-greitens/.

149. "Red's Giant Hamburg." Wikipedia. Wikimedia Foundation, May 30, 2020. https://en.wikipedia.org/wiki/Red's_Giant_Hamburg.

150. Reimann, Matt. "In One Year, 12 Trillion Locusts Devastated the Great Plains-and Then They Went Extinct." Medium. Timeline, February 16, 2017. https://timeline.com/in-the-1870s-12-trillion-locusts-devastated-the-great-plains-and-then-they-went-extinct-6f7c51a15d90.

151. Keeven-Franke, D. (2016, August 10). St. Charles County History. Retrieved January 02, 2021, from https://stcharlescountyhistory.org/2016/08/10/statehood/

152. 1888 Democratic National Convention. (2020, December 03). Retrieved January 02, 2021, from https://en.wikipedia.org/wiki/1888_Democratic_National_Convention

153. "The Civil War in Missouri." Constitution of 1865—Drake Constitution | The Civil War in Missouri. The Missouri History Museum. Accessed October 14, 2020. http://www.civilwarmo.org/educators/resources/info-sheets/constitution-1865-drake-constitution.

154. "Platte Purchase." Wikipedia. Wikimedia Foundation, December 25, 2020. https://en.wikipedia.org/wiki/Platte_Purchase.

155. Garau, Annie. "The Strange Tale Of The Smallest Player In Major League History." All That's Interesting. All That's Interesting, June 24, 2020. https://allthatsinteresting.com/eddie-gaedel-shortest-baseball-player.

156. "Springfield Public Square." The Library. Springfield-Greene County Library. Accessed April 2, 1999. https://thelibrary.org/lochist/postcards/public_square.cfm.

157. "Discover Arrow Rock." The Village of Arrow Rock. Village of Arrow Rock. Accessed September 28, 2020. https://arrowrock.org/about-discover-arrow-rock/.

158. Scott, A. O. "Where Life Is Cold, and Kin Are Cruel." *The New York Times. The New York Times*, June 10, 2010. https://www.nytimes.com/2010/06/11/movies/11winter.html.

159. Rehagen, Tony. "A Look Back at the Blues' Epic Run Leading up to Game 7 of the Stanley Cup Final." *St. Louis Magazine*, June 12, 2019. https://www.stlmag.com/news/sports/the-blues-gloria-stanley-cup-final-team-of-the-year/.

160. Grubbs, Brian. "Here Is What Happened This Week in Ozarks History." Leader. News-Leader, June 11, 2017. https://www.news-leader.com/story/news/local/ozarks/2017/06/11/here-what-happened-week-ozarks-history/380849001/.

161. "Kansas City (Leiber and Stoller Song)." Wikipedia. Wikimedia Foundation, December 12, 2020. https://en.wikipedia.org/wiki/Kansas_City_(Leiber_and_Stoller_song).

162. "1947: Sam Snead Misses 30 in Putt on Final Hole, Lew Worsham Wins." Golf History Today, June 15, 2019. https://golfhistorytoday.com/1947-lew-worsham-sam-snead/.

163. Davis, Elizabeth. "HISTORICALLY YOURS: Official Symbols for Missouri." *Boonville Daily News*—Boonville, MO. *Boonville Daily News*, Boonville, MO, September 20, 2019. https://www.boonvilledailynews.com/news/20190920/historically-yours-official-symbols-for-missouri.

164. "Kansas City Massacre 'Pretty Boy' Floyd." FBI. FBI, May 18, 2016. https://www.fbi.gov/history/famous-cases/kansas-city-massacre-pretty-boy-floyd.

165. "Ste. Genevieve, Missouri." Wikipedia. Wikimedia Foundation, December 6, 2020. https://en.wikipedia.org/wiki/Ste._Genevieve,_Missouri.

166. Brown, John. "Charles Leiper Grigg: Missouri Business Legend." Missouri Legends, June 17, 2010. https://missourilegends.com/missouri-business-legends/charles-leiper-grigg/.

167. "History—Truman State University." Truman State University, December 11, 2020. https://www.truman.edu/about/history/.

168. Brown, John. *Missouri: An Illustrated Timeline*. St. Louis, MO: Reedy Press, 2020.

169. "Osteopathic Medicine Turns 137!" A. T. Still University, June 30, 2011. https://iconnect.atsu.edu/osteopathic-medicine-turns-137.

170. Schmidt, Daniel. "If You Shoot a Compound Bow, Thank This Man." Deer and Deer Hunting, March 5, 2020. https://www.deeranddeerhunting.com/content/blogs/dan-schmidt-deer-blog-whitetail-wisdom/if-you-shoot-a-compound-bow-thank-this-man/.

171. "Forest Park Timeline." Forest Park Forever. Accessed November 24, 2020. https://www.forestparkforever.org/park-timeline.

172. "Walk of Fame." St. Louis Walk of Fame. Accessed January 3, 2021. http://stlouiswalkoffame. org/.

173. "Genome Announcement a Milestone, but Only a Beginning." CNN.com, June 26, 2000. https:// www.cnn.com/2000/HEALTH/06/26/human.genome.05/index.html.

174. Emery, Tom. "Flooded with Memories: Recollections of Devastating Summer of 1993 Linger, 25 Years Later." Courier. Jacksonville Journal-Courier, July 30, 2018. https://www.myjournalcourier. com/news/article/Flooded-with-memories-Recollections-of-13115701.php.

175. Kohler, Jeremy, and Laurie Skrivan. "The St. Louis Couple Charged with Waving Guns at Protesters Have a Long History of Not Backing Down." STLtoday.com, November 7, 2020. https://www.stltoday.com/news/local/metro/the-st-louis-couple-charged-with-waving-guns-at-protesters-have-a-long-history-of/article_281d9989-373e-53c3-abcb-ecd0225dd287.html.

176. "The Game of Their Lives (2005 Film)." Wikipedia. Wikimedia Foundation, July 14, 2020. https://en.wikipedia.org/wiki/The_Game_of_Their_Lives_(2005_film).

177. Missouri Secretary of State—IT. "State Symbols of Missouri." Official State of Missouri Web Site. Missouri Secretary of State's Office. Accessed January 3, 2021. https://www.sos.mo.gov/symbol/ song.

178. "School of Medicine." UMKC School of Medicine. Accessed October 3, 2020. https://med.umkc. edu/em/history/.

179. Yates, Henry. "Bikers, Fire Hoses and Looting: The Story of the Guns N' Roses Fan Riot in St. Louis." Classic Rock Magazine. Future Publishing, September 8, 2019. https://www.loudersound. com/features/bikers-fire-hoses-and-looting-the-story-of-the-guns-n-roses-fan-riot-in-st-louis.

180. "About." Fair Saint Louis, May 26, 2020. https://www.fairsaintlouis.org/about/.

181. Binkovitz, Leah. "From Virginia to Missouri to the Smithsonian: Jefferson's Tombstone Has a Long Story." Smithsonian.com. Smithsonian Institution, February 15, 2013. https://www. smithsonianmag.com/smithsonian-institution/from-virginia-to-missouri-to-the-smithsonian-jeffersons-tombstone-has-a-long-story-18782980/.

182. "Dwight F. Davis." Encyclopedia Britannica. Encyclopedia Britannica, inc., November 24, 2020. https://www.britannica.com/biography/Dwight-F-Davis.

183. Norcross, Amy. "Sliced Bread Is Sold for the 1st Time, July 7, 1928." EDN. Aspencore Network, July 6, 2020. https://www.edn.com/sliced-bread-is-sold-for-the-1st-time-july-7-1928/.

184. Cardarella, Tony. "The Long-Awaited Jackson Brothers 'Victory Tour' Opened Friday Night..." UPI. United Press International, July 6, 1984. https://www.upi.com/Archives/1984/07/06/The-long-awaited-Jackson-brothers-Victory-Tour-opened-Friday-night/1069457934400/.

185. Spencer, Kaye. "A Brief History of the Corncob Pipe." Wester Fictioneers, July 9, 2018. https:// westernfictioneers.blogspot.com/2018/07/a-brief-history-of-corncob-pipe-by-kaye.html.

186. Dalbey, Beth. "Who Killed Ken Rex McElroy: Town Keeps Its Secret For 38 Years." Across America, US Patch. Patch, August 26, 2019. https://patch.com/us/across-america/who-killed-ken-rex-mcelroy-town-keeps-its-secret-38-years.

187. Stiles, Nancy. "The Long and Tangled History of Norton, Missouri's State Grape." Feast Magazine. Feast Media, June 5, 2019. https://www.feastmagazine.com/drink/features/ article_01a36b3e-47da-11e8-bc15-17c258412c5f.html.

188. "2009 Major League Baseball All-Star Game." Wikipedia. Wikimedia Foundation, December 16, 2020. https://en.wikipedia.org/wiki/2009_Major_League_Baseball_All-Star_Game.

189. "Trans World Airlines." Wikipedia. Wikimedia Foundation, December 18, 2020. https:// en.wikipedia.org/wiki/Trans_World_Airlines.

190. "George Washington Carver National Monument (US National Park Service)." National Parks Service. US Department of the Interior. Accessed December 15, 2020. https://www.nps.gov/ places/george-washington-carver-national-monument.htm.

191. "Robert Stroud." Encyclopedia Britannica. Encyclopedia Britannica, inc., January 1, 2021. https://www.britannica.com/biography/Robert-Stroud.

192. Russell, Greta. "Ginger Rogers." Missouri Women, December 7, 2010. https://missouriwomen. org/2010/12/03/ginger-rogers/.

193. McFadden, Christopher. "Understanding the Tragic Hyatt Regency Walkway Collapse." Interesting Engineering. Interesting Engineering, March 12, 2018. https:// interestingengineering.com/understanding-hyatt-regency-walkway-collapse.

194. "About Margaret 'Molly' Brown." Molly Brown House Museum, April 25, 2020. https:// mollybrown.org/about-molly-brown/.

195. Schneider, Joey. "Duck Boat Tragedy: Sunday Marks Two Years since Duck Boat Capsized on Table Rock Lake, 17 Killed." https://www.ky3.com, July 19, 2020. https://www.ky3.com/2020/07/19/sunday-marks-the-two-year-anniversary-of-the-duck-boat-sinking-on-table-rock-lake/.

196. "Red Crown Tourist Court." Wikipedia. Wikimedia Foundation, June 14, 2020. https://en.wikipedia.org/wiki/Red_Crown_Tourist_Court.

197. "Wild Bill's Shootout." Wild Bill's Shootout | Springfield, MO—Official Website. Accessed January 4, 2021. https://www.springfieldmo.gov/1839/Wild-Bill-Hickoks-Shootout-on-the-Square.

198. "A. P. Green (1875 – 1956)." A. P. Green—Historic Missourians—The State Historical Society of Missouri. Accessed November 8, 2020. https://historicmissourians.shsmo.org/historicmissourians/name/g/green/.

199. Wancho, Joseph. "July 23, 2009: Mark Buehrle Throws a Perfect Game for White Sox." Society for American Baseball Research, April 17, 2020. https://sabr.org/gamesproj/game/july-23-2009-mark-buehrle-throws-a-perfect-game-for-white-sox/.

200. "Christopher S. Bond Bridge (Hermann, Missouri)." Wikiwand. Accessed January 3, 2021. https://www.wikiwand.com/en/Christopher_S._Bond_Bridge_(Hermann,_Missouri).

201. Chesterton, Eric Twitter icon Email icon. "The 'Pine Tar Incident' Remains One of the Craziest Stories Baseball Has Ever Told." MLB.com, July 24, 2018. https://www.mlb.com/cut4/what-is-the-pine-tar-game-c286938216.

202. "July 25, 1972: VP Nominee, Missouri Sen. Thomas Eagleton Discloses Electric Shock Treatments." STLtoday.com. *St. Louis Post-Dispatch*, July 25, 2020. https://www.stltoday.com/news/local/history/july-25-1972-vp-nominee-missouri-sen-thomas-eagleton-discloses-electric-shock-treatments/article_09e6dadc-7531-5553-8e9b-e3f07870fea1.html.

203. "History of St. Joseph." St. Joseph, MO—Official Website. City of St. Joseph, Missouri. Accessed January 4, 2021. https://www.stjoemo.info/151/History-of-St-Joseph.

204. "The Death of Jesse James." PBS. Public Broadcasting Service. Accessed January 4, 2021. https://www.pbs.org/wgbh/americanexperience/features/james-death/.

205. O'Connor, Patrick. "Debate on Ice-Cream Cone's Origins Rages Hot and Cold." chicagotribune.com. Chicago Tribune, August 27, 2018. https://www.chicagotribune.com/news/ct-xpm-2004-04-15-0404150073-story.html.

206. "Casey Stengel." Baseball Hall of Fame. Accessed January 5, 2021. https://baseballhall.org/hall-of-famers/stengel-casey.

207. "Two Historical 1981 Corvettes: The First and Last." Vette-Vues. Vette Vues Magazine, July 14, 2020. https://vette-vues.com/two-historical-1981-corvettes-the-first-and-last/.

208. "Rush Limbaugh." Encyclopedia Britannica. Encyclopedia Britannica, inc. Accessed November 19, 2020. https://www.britannica.com/biography/Rush-Limbaugh.

209. "Palmyra Spectator to Stop Printing Oct. 31." Herald-Whig, October 30, 2020. https://www.whig.com/archive/article/palmyra-spectator-to-stop-printing-oct-31/article_d23c0335-6ffa-529c-9dec-3ab90ed2058d.html.

210. NIHF Inductee William Lear Invented the Car Radio. Accessed October 5, 2020. https://www.invent.org/inductees/william-p-lear.

211. "Helen Stephens (1918–1994)." Historic Missourians. The State Historical Society of Missouri. Accessed November 26, 2020. https://historicmissourians.shsmo.org/historicmissourians/name/s/stephens/.

212. "Hallmark History: Hallmark Corporate Information." Hallmark Corporate, December 31, 2019. https://corporate.hallmark.com/about/hallmark-cards-company/history/.

213. Gillespie, Michael. "Bagnell Dam Facts and Figures." Bagnell Dam Facts, 2005. http://www.lakehistory.info/damfacts.html.

214. "James Eads Timeline." PBS. Public Broadcasting Service. Accessed December 24, 2020. https://www.pbs.org/wgbh/americanexperience/features/eads-james-eads-timeline/.

215. "President Truman Signs United Nations Charter." History.com. A&E Television Networks, November 13, 2009. https://www.history.com/this-day-in-history/truman-signs-united-nations-charter.

216. Lowery, Wesley, and Mark Berman. "The 12 Key Highlights from the DOJ's Scathing Ferguson Report." *The Washington Post*. WP Company, April 27, 2019. https://www.washingtonpost.com/news/post-nation/wp/2015/03/04/the-12-key-highlights-from-the-dojs-scathing-ferguson-report/.

217. Missouri Became the 24th State. Library of Congress. Accessed January 6, 2021. http://www.americaslibrary.gov/jb/nation/jb_nation_missouri_2.html.

218. "Omar Nelson Bradley." Encyclopedia Britannica. Encyclopedia Britannica, inc. Accessed October 15, 2020. https://www.britannica.com/biography/Omar-Nelson-Bradley.

219. "Porter Wagoner." Country Music Hall of Fame, September 30, 2020. https://countrymusichalloffame.org/artist/porter-wagoner/.

220. "Three States Claim First Interstate Highway." US Department of Transportation/Federal Highway Administration. Accessed January 6, 2021. https://www.fhwa.dot.gov/publications/publicroads/96summer/p96su18.cfm.

221. "Pitching Ace Bob Gibson Throws First No-Hitter." History.com. A&E Television Networks, November 16, 2009. https://www.history.com/this-day-in-history/pitching-ace-throws-first-no-hitter.

222. McConnell, Kaitlyn. "Springfield's Cobra Scare of 1953." Ozarks Alive, March 22, 2020. https://ozarksalive.com/orlandos-lost-cobra-causes-60-year-flashback/.

223. "Bernarr Macfadden." Encyclopedia Britannica. Encyclopedia Britannica, inc. Accessed October 6, 2020. https://www.britannica.com/biography/Bernarr-Macfadden.

224. "History of Anheuser." Building an American Icon. Anheuser Busch. Accessed November 22, 2020. https://www.anheuser-busch.com/about/heritage.html.

225. "Climatron Conservatory." Climatron History and Architecture. Missouri Botanical Garden. Accessed January 7, 2021. http://www.mobot.org/hort/gardens/CLhistarchit.shtml.

226. "This Day in St. Louis History, August 19, 1877." St. Louis, MO, August 19, 2013. https://www.facebook.com/GatewayArchNPS/posts/a-river-monster-in-st-louis-a-fun-story-from-stl250s-page-jrc/491286294296303/.

227. McGuire, John. "25 Years Ago: The Coral Court Closed Its Doors for the Final Time." STLtoday.com. *St. Louis Post-Dispatch*, April 22, 2020. https://www.stltoday.com/news/archives/25-years-ago-the-coral-court-closed-its-doors-for-the-final-time/article_13cc3396-c99c-5c44-854c-3f7061133c4f.html.

228. "Washington County, Missouri." Familypedia. Wikia.Org. Accessed January 6, 2021. https://familypedia.wikia.org/wiki/Washington_County,_Missouri#:~:text=As%20of%20the%202010%20census,President%20of%20the%20United%20States.

229. O'Neil, Tim. "Aug. 22, 1876 • How the 'Great Divorce' of St. Louis City and St. Louis County Started." STLtoday.com. *St. Louis Post-Dispatch*, August 23, 2020. https://www.stltoday.com/news/local/history/aug-22-1876-how-the-great-divorce-of-st-louis-city-and-st-louis-county/article_3e93fa29-7d01-570d-94f2-31eca08a9378.html#:~:text=22%2C%201876%2C%20voters%20in%20St,lost%20badly%20in%20the%20county.

230. Ballentine, Summer. "Science Fiction Author Heinlein Honored as Famous Missourian." newstribune.com. Jefferson City News Tribune, August 23, 2016. https://www.newstribune.com/news/missouri/story/2016/aug/23/science-fiction-author-heinlein-honored-famous-missourian/636992/.

231. "Stephens College." Wikipedia. Wikimedia Foundation, October 12, 2020. https://en.wikipedia.org/wiki/Stephens_College.

232. "St. Louis, Missouri Population History 1840–2019." St. Louis, Missouri Population History | 1840–2019. Biggest Cities.com, November 18, 2020. https://www.biggestuscities.com/city/st-louis-missouri.

233. "Was the Nation's First Kindergarten in St. Louis?" *St. Louis Magazine*, August 25, 2017. https://www.stlmag.com/history/st-louis-sage/was-the-first-kindergarten-in-st-louis/.

234. Larsen, Thomas B. "From Pioneer Forest to Political Prop: Power Geographies of the Ozark National Scenic Riverways." Artifacts Journal. University of Missouri, August 2014. https://artifactsjournal.missouri.edu/2014/08/from-pioneer-forest-to-political-prop-power-geographies-of-the-ozark-national-scenic-riverways/.

235. "1820 Missouri Gubernatorial Election." Wikipedia. Wikimedia Foundation, December 31, 2020. https://en.wikipedia.org/wiki/1820_Missouri_gubernatorial_election#:~:text=The%20Missouri%20gubernatorial%20election%20of,was%20defeated%20by%20Alexander%20McNair.

236. Andrews, Evan. "8 Unusual Facts About the 1904 St. Louis Olympics." History.com. A&E Television Networks, August 29, 2014. https://www.history.com/news/8-unusual-facts-about-the-1904-st-louis-olympics.

237. Andrews, Evan. "8 Unusual Facts About the 1904 St. Louis Olympics." History.com. A&E Television Networks, August 29, 2014. https://www.history.com/news/8-unusual-facts-about-the-1904-st-louis-olympics.

238. "Marie Byrum Transcript." Missouri State Archives. Missouri Secretary of State. Accessed January 7, 2021. https://www.sos.mo.gov/mdh/MMH/transcripts/mmph_tsByrum.

239. "How A St. Louis Icon Keeps Reinventing Itself." St. Louis Union Station. Accessed September 14, 2020. https://www.stlouisunionstation.com/story.

240. "Eugene Field." Encyclopedia Britannica. Encyclopedia Britannica, inc., November 14, 2020. https://www.britannica.com/biography/Eugene-Field.

241. Allen, Kelsey. "Champion of the Comics." Show Me Mizzou. University of Missouri, April 20, 2018. https://showme.missouri.edu/2018/champion-of-the-comics/.

242. James, Marquis. Essay. In *The Life of Andrew Jackson*, 152–54. Indianapolis, IN: Bobbs-Merrill, 1938. http://www.adena.com/adena/usa/hs/hs23.htm.

243. Gregorian, Vahe. "Football's Forward Pass Started with an Innovator at St. Louis University." STLtoday.com. *St. Louis Post-Dispatch*, September 5, 2020. https://www.stltoday.com/sports/college/slu/footballs-forward-pass-started-with-an-innovator-at-st-louis-university/article_cb3c85c4-eeeb-11ea-9fcb-bb05a9a5fe78.html.

244. "2009 Tour of Missouri." Wikipedia. Wikimedia Foundation, January 29, 2020. https://en.wikipedia.org/wiki/2009_Tour_of_Missouri.

245. Justice, Richard. "McGwire Surpasses Maris With 62nd Home Run." *The Washington Post*. WP Company, September 8, 1998. https://www.washingtonpost.com/wp-srv/sports/baseball/longterm/chase/articles/mac9.htm.

246. "Fair History." Missouri State Fair. Accessed January 7, 2021. https://www.mostatefair.com/fair-history/.

247. "The Great St. Louis Bank Robbery." Wikipedia. Wikimedia Foundation, December 4, 2020. https://en.wikipedia.org/wiki/The_Great_St._Louis_Bank_Robbery.

248. Holleman, Joe. "Spotlight: Grand Center, Home to Theaters and First Drive-Thru." STLtoday.com. *St. Louis Post-Dispatch*, May 13, 2018. https://www.stltoday.com/news/local/columns/joe-holleman/spotlight-grand-center-home-to-theaters-and-first-drive-thru/article_10057b9e-6b47-5996-ac7c-9048e93f0f40.html.

249. "Dale Carnegie (1888–1955)." Historic Missourians. The State Historical Society of Missouri, November 7, 2020. https://historicmissourians.shsmo.org/historicmissourians/name/c/carnegie/.

250. "Bob Barker, Famous Missourian." Missourinet, September 13, 2007. https://www.missourinet.com/2007/09/13/bob-barker-famous-missourian/.

251. O'Neil, Tim, and Mitch Smith. "Former St. Louis Officer, Jason Stockley, Acquitted in Shooting of Black Driver." *The New York Times*. The New York Times, September 15, 2017. https://www.nytimes.com/2017/09/15/us/jason-stockley-anthony-lamar-smith-st-louis-officer.html.

252. Cohen, Howard. "How 'Miami Vice' Changed TV." miamiherald. Miami Herald, September 17, 2018. https://www.miamiherald.com/entertainment/tv/article2261012.html.

253. "Our History." Lincoln University, October 3, 2020. https://www.lincolnu.edu/web/about-lincoln/our-history.

254. The Kansas City Star. "Our History." Kansascity.com. The Kansas City Star. Accessed January 7, 2021. https://www.kansascity.com/customer-service/about-us/article7944.html.

255. Gooden, Joe. "Day off in Alton, Missouri." The Beatles Bible. The Beatles Bible, September 15, 2016. https://www.beatlesbible.com/1964/09/19/day-off-alton-missouri/.

256. "Sheryl Crow." Wikipedia. Wikimedia Foundation, December 27, 2020. https://en.wikipedia.org/wiki/Sheryl_Crow.

257. O'Neil, Tim. "Hazelwood Ford Plant Was the Centerpiece of Muscular Postwar Expansion." STLtoday.com. *St. Louis Post-Dispatch*, April 22, 2020. https://www.stltoday.com/business/local/hazelwood-ford-plant-was-the-centerpiece-of-muscular-postwar-expansion/article_e9c2c6bd-a144-5c74-840d-f1ca593c4bb6.html.

258. Lear, Mike. "Historian, Former Inmate, Troopers Recall 1954 MO Penitentiary Riot." Missourinet. Learfield News, October 9, 2014. https://www.missourinet.com/2014/09/22/historian-and-former-inmate-troopers-recall-mo-penitentiary-riot-of-1954/.

259. "Theodore Roosevelt in the Missouri Ozarks." BuffaloReflex.com. The Buffalo Reflex, November 20, 2014. https://buffaloreflex.com/heritage/theodore-roosevelt-in-the-missouri-ozarks/article_72418c04-6e76-11e4-a5f4-d772d61e1a1c.html.

260. Mosley, Jim. "High-Speed Train to KC Studied." *St. Louis Post-Dispatch*, September 24, 1987, sec. A. p. 1

261. "Michael S. Hopkins." Wikipedia. Wikimedia Foundation, January 5, 2021. https://en.wikipedia.org/wiki/Michael_S._Hopkins.

262. "The Bass Pro Shops Story—Bass Pro." *Bass Pro*, January 5, 2021. about.basspro.com/.

263. Wolnisty, Claire. "Centralia Massacre." Civil War on the Western Border: The Missouri-Kansas Conflict, 1854-1865. Kansas City Public Library. Accessed November 6, 2020. civilwaronthewesternborder.org/encyclopedia/centralia-massacre.

264. "A Byte Out of History: The Bobby Greenlease Kidnapping," September 30, 2013. https://www.fbi.gov/news/stories/a-byte-out-of-history-the-bobby-greenlease-kidnapping1.

265. Pokin, Steve. "Pokin Around: The Day a Truck Full of Dynamite Exploded on I-44." NewsLeader.com. Springfield News-Leader, February 27, 2017. https://www.news-leader.com/story/news/local/ozarks/2017/02/24/pokin-around-day-truck-full-dynamite-exploded--44/98307336/.

266. "Timeline of Missouri History: 1800-1820." Missouri Digital Heritage. Missouri Secretary of State. Accessed October 22, 2020. https://www.sos.mo.gov/archives/history/timeline/timeline2.

267. Glass, Andrew, and Annie Karni. "Joe Biden and Sarah Palin Debate, Oct. 2, 2008." POLITICO, October 2, 2017. https://www.politico.com/story/2017/10/02/joe-biden-and-sarah-palin-debate-oct-2-2008-243348.

268. "Gone Girl (Film)." Wikipedia. Wikimedia Foundation, December 27, 2020. https://en.wikipedia.org/wiki/Gone_Girl_(film).

269. Walls, Kathleen. "Frank – The Other James Boy." Legends of America. Accessed January 8, 2021. https://www.legendsofamerica.com/we-frankjames/#:~:text=On%20October%205%2C%201882%2C%20he,and%20murder%20of%20Joseph%20Heywood.

270. "Thomas Akers." Wikipedia. Wikimedia Foundation, October 28, 2020. https://en.wikipedia.org/wiki/Thomas_Akers.

271. Marshall, Colin. "Pruitt-Igoe: The Troubled High-Rise That Came to Define Urban America – a History of Cities in 50 Buildings, Day 21." The Guardian. Guardian News and Media, April 22, 2015. https://www.theguardian.com/cities/2015/apr/22/pruitt-igoe-high-rise-urban-america-history-cities.

272. "Kay Thompson." Wikipedia. Wikimedia Foundation, January 7, 2021. https://en.wikipedia.org/wiki/Kay_Thompson.

273. "1944 World Series." Wikipedia. Wikimedia Foundation, October 29, 2020. https://en.wikipedia.org/wiki/1944_World_Series.

274. "History: A Look Back into the History of OEF." Ozark Empire Fairgrounds & Event Center. Ozark Empire Fair. Accessed January 8, 2021. https://www.ozarkempirefair.com/p/about/history.

275. "Redd Foxx." Encyclopedia Britannica. Encyclopedia Britannica, inc., December 5, 2020. https://www.britannica.com/biography/Redd-Foxx#:~:text=Redd%20Foxx%2C%20original%20name%20John,matter%2C%20influenced%20generations%20of%20comics.

276. Edgell, Holly. "'A Monumental Figure:' 4 Times Martin Luther King Jr. Spoke in St. Louis." St. Louis Public Radio, January 16, 2018. https://news.stlpublicradio.org/arts/2018-01-14/a-monumental-figure-4-times-martin-luther-king-jr-spoke-in-st-louis.

277. Van Brunt, Henry. "When Priests of Pallas Made the City Festive." *Kansas City Times*, October 17, 1963.

278. Hummel, Rick. "35 Years Ago: Ozzie Smith's 3,000-to-1 Shot Made St. Louis 'Go Crazy.'" STLtoday.com. *St. Louis Post-Dispatch*, October 22, 2020. https://www.stltoday.com/sports/baseball/professional/35-years-ago-ozzie-smiths-3-000-to-1-shot-made-st-louis-go-crazy/article_893d3eba-d8ae-11df-9afe-0017a4a78c22.html#:~:text=Louis%20'Go%20Crazy',-By%20Rick%20Hummel&text=On%20Oct.,a%20Hall%20of%20Fame%20announcer.

279. "UMSL Takes Parts in Moratorium." *UMSL Current*. October 16, 1969, Vol 4, No 5 edition.

280. "Remembering Gov. Mel Carnahan – 19 Years after Deadly Plane Crash." STLtoday.com. St. Louis Post Dispatch.com, October 15, 2020. https://www.stltoday.com/news/multimedia/remembering-gov-mel-carnahan-19-years-after-deadly-plane-crash/collection_7212a399-2fed-5d0e-be70-6ac7f98385f3.html.

281. Wuellner, Jean. "Last Cattle Auction at KC Stockyards." KansasCity.com. The Kansas City Star, September 27, 1991. https://www.kansascity.com/latest-news/article295396/Last-cattle-auction-at-KC-stockyards.html.

282. "Cathedral Basilica Celebrates Its 100th." Explore St. Louis. St. Louis Convention & Visitors Commission, September 2, 2014. https://explorestlouis.com/cathedral-basilica-celebrates/.

283. "White Palace (Film)." Wikipedia. Wikimedia Foundation, December 4, 2020. https://en.wikipedia.org/wiki/White_Palace_(film).

284. "The Senate Approves for Ratification the Louisiana Purchase Treaty." US Senate: Art and History. United States Senate, July 15, 2020. https://www.senate.gov/about/powers-procedures/treaties/senate-approves-louisiana-purchase-treaty.htm.

285. Pryor, Joe. "Progress Notes: Ha Ha Tonka History." MillerCountyMuseum.org. Miller County Museum & Historical Society, September 6, 2010. http://www.millercountymuseum.org/archives/100906.html.

286. O'Neil, Tim. "Heist Reminiscent of Unsolved Brinks Robbery Here." STLtoday.com. *St. Louis Post-Dispatch*, December 18, 2012. https://www.stltoday.com/news/local/crime-and-courts/heist-reminiscent-of-unsolved-brinks-robbery-here/article_7ec83fee-9bfc-566e-924b-a039663369ad.html.

287. Sonderman, Joe. Essay. In *St. Louis 365: Intriguing Events From Each Day of the Year!* 209. St. Louis, MO: Stellar Press, 2002.

288. Moriarty, Jim. "10-25-99: Revisiting the Day Payne Stewart Died." Golf Digest. Golf Digest, October 25, 2019. https://www.golfdigest.com/story/golf-payne-stewart-moriarty-1005.

289. "October 26, 1985: Royals Force Game 7 after Cardinals' Collapse in Wake of Denkinger's Call." Sabr.com. Society for American Baseball Research, October 26, 2020. https://sabr.org/gamesproj/game/october-26-1985-royals-force-game-7-after-cardinals-collapse-in-wake-of-denkingers-call/.

290. Pokin, Steve. "Pokin Around: Was There Ever a Time in Missouri When You Could Legally Kill a Mormon?" News-Leader. Springfield News-Leader, September 2, 2018. https://www.news-leader.com/story/news/local/ozarks/2018/09/01/missouri-executive-order-44-mormon-war/1147461002/.

291. "St. Louis's Gateway Arch Is Completed." History.com. A&E Television Networks, November 24, 2009. https://www.history.com/this-day-in-history/gateway-arch-completed#:~:text=On%20October%2028%2C%201965%2C%20construction,Louis%2C%20Missouri.

292. "Kansas City Union Station." Wikipedia. Wikimedia Foundation, January 3, 2021. https://en.wikipedia.org/wiki/Kansas_City_Union_Station.

293. Pollock, Bill. "Mizzou vs KU Football Is Back, but You'll Have to Wait a Few Years." Missourinet. Learfield News, May 2, 2020. https://www.missourinet.com/2020/05/02/mizzou-vs-ku-football-is-back-but-youll-have-to-wait-a-few-years/.

294. Ham, Ray. "Gasconade Bridge Disaster: The Immediate Aftermath Nov. 1, 1855-Nov. 5, 1855." The Hermann Advertiser Courier, June 16, 2020. https://www.hermannadvertisercourier.com/living/gasconade-bridge-disaster-the-immediate-aftermath-nov-1-1855-nov-5-1855/article_e01f1b7e-b001-11ea-b455-4bf62fe9fe27.html.

295. "Shrine Mosque History." Shrine Mosque. Shrine Mosque History & Preservation Association. Accessed January 8, 2021. https://www.abashrine.com/shrine-mosque.html.

296. O'Neil, Tim. "Marine Sgt. Rocky Sickmann Returns Home from Iran to Cheers, Ribbons." STLtoday.com. *St. Louis Post-Dispatch*, April 22, 2020. https://www.stltoday.com/news/archives/a-look-back-marine-sgt-rocky-sickmann-returns-home-from-iran-to-cheers-ribbons/article_21229a28-4e62-5df0-887c-c62808da40f0.html.

297. "Excelsior Springs, Missouri." Wikipedia. Wikimedia Foundation, January 4, 2021. https://en.wikipedia.org/wiki/Excelsior_Springs,_Missouri.

298. "History of the Missouri Lottery." MO Lottery. Missouri Lottery. Accessed January 8, 2021. http://www.molottery.com/learnaboutus/history.shtm.

299. DeRiso, Nick. "Doobie Brothers Officially Join the Rock and Roll Hall of Fame." Ultimate Classic Rock. Ultimate Classic Rock, November 8, 2020. https://ultimateclassicrock.com/doobie-brothers-rock-hall-induction/.

300. Rutherford, John. "Springfield's Hospital With a Soul." *Fifty Plus*, February 2002. Published electronically by Springfield-Greene County Library. https://thelibrary.org/lochist/oreilly/fiftyplus.cfm

301. "McDonnell Douglas AV-8B Harrier II." Wikipedia. Wikimedia Foundation, December 28, 2020. https://en.wikipedia.org/wiki/McDonnell_Douglas_AV-8B_Harrier_II.

302. "Jane Froman (1907 – 1980)." Jane Froman—Historic Missourians. The State Historical Society of Missouri. Accessed January 8, 2021. https://historicmissourians.shsmo.org/historicmissourians/name/f/froman/.

303. Roe, Jason. "Plane Speaking." KC History. Kansas City Public Library. Accessed January 10, 2021. https://kchistory.org/week-kansas-city-history/plane-speaking.

304. Jacob, Jerry. "FLASHBACK: Brad Pitt Attends Premiere of 'Meet Joe Black' at Springfield's Campbell 16 Cine." KY3.com. Gray Media Group, March 16, 2016. https://www.ky3.com/content/news/FLASHBACK-Brad-Pitt-attends-premiere-of-Meet-Joe-Black-at-Springfields-Campbell-16-Cine-379683181.html.

305. Walker, Malea. "How Newspapers Helped Crowdsource a Scientific Discovery: The 1833 Leonid Meteor Storm." Headlines and Heroes. Library of Congress, September 2, 2020. https://blogs.loc.gov/headlinesandheroes/2020/09/how-newspapers-helped-crowdsource-a-scientific-discovery-the-1833-leonid-meteor-storm/#:~:text=The%20Leonid%20meteor%20storm%20was,know%20more%20about%20this%20phenomenon.

306. Vintage St. Louis & Route 66. Facebook. Accessed January 8, 2021. https://www.facebook.com/permalink.php?story_fbid=2638130779567132&id=513201722060059&comment_id=2638349516211925&reply_comment_id=2638512469528963.

307. "Phog Allen." Encyclopedia Britannica. Encyclopedia Britannica, inc., November 11, 2020. https://www.britannica.com/biography/Phog-Allen.

308. "John B. Henderson." Wikipedia. Wikimedia Foundation, January 7, 2021. https://en.wikipedia.org/wiki/John_B._Henderson.

309. Lee, Janice. "Biography of Benoist Troost (1786-1859), Physician and Early Settler." Kansas City, 2003. https://kchistory.org/islandora/object/kchistory%253A115405.

310. Trammell, Kendall. "6 Mickey Mouse Facts You Probably Didn't Know." CNN. Cable News Network, November 18, 2017. https://www.cnn.com/2017/11/18/entertainment/mickey-mouse-fun-facts-trivia-trnd/index.html#:~:text=Mickey%20Mouse%20first%20debuted%20in,%22%20on%20November%2018%2C%201928.

311. "The Rolling Stones American Tour 1981." Wikipedia. Wikimedia Foundation, December 4, 2020. https://en.wikipedia.org/wiki/The_Rolling_Stones_American_Tour_1981.

312. Corry, John. "TV View; 'The Day After': Tv As A Rallying Cry." *New York Times*. November 20, 1983, sec. 2. p 1

313. "Jim Davis (Actor)." Wikipedia. Wikimedia Foundation, December 22, 2020. https://en.wikipedia.org/wiki/Jim_Davis_(actor).

314. "Meet Me in St. Louis." Encyclopedia Britannica. Encyclopedia Britannica, inc. Accessed January 10, 2021. https://www.britannica.com/topic/Meet-Me-in-St-Louis.

315. Missouri University of Science and Technology. "History Of Missouri University Of Science And Technology." Missouri S&T. Curators of the University of Missouri. Accessed October 10, 2020. https://chancellor.mst.edu/history/.

316. O'Connor, W.J. "'Much Music, near Riots and Singing'—Looking Back at the Mizzou Game That Started Homecoming." STLtoday.com, November 25, 2020. https://www.stltoday.com/sports/college/mizzou/much-music-near-riots-and-singing---looking-back-at-the-mizzou-game-that/article_0b16021d-a66a-5515-8739-723bb8139ad1.html.

317. "Louisiana Purchase Exposition." TR Center. Theodore Roosevelt Center. Accessed January 10, 2021. https://www.theodorerooseveltcenter.org/Learn-About-TR/TR-Encyclopedia/Culture-and-Society/Louisiana-Purchase-Exposition.

318. "Mizzourah! Football at MU: The Early Years." University Archives. University of Missouri, March 20, 2003. https://muarchives.missouri.edu/football2.html.

319. Rotermund, Maggie. "SLU Legends and Lore: The Billiken Soccer Dynasty." Saint Louis University, September 27, 2019. https://www.slu.edu/news/2019/september/slu-legends-lore-soccer.php#:~:text=With%20Bob%20Guelker%20as%20an,2%20in%20the%20championship%20game.

320. Burke, Robert. "Hazmat Studies: Kansas City's Darkest Day." Firehouse. Endeavor Business Media, November 1, 2018. https://www.firehouse.com/rescue/hazardous-materials/article/21021866/30-years-later-kansas-city-explosion-firehouse-magazine.

321. Leiser, Ken. "State Drops Klan from Trash Pickup Program." *St. Louis Post-Dispatch*. 5 April 2001 (p. C1).

322. "Annexation of Westport by Kansas City." KC History. Kansas City Public Library. Accessed January 11, 2021. https://kchistory.org/islandora/object/kchistory%3A75815?solr_nav%5Bid%5D=027985822bfa9508495e&solr_nav%5Bpage%5D=4&solr_nav%5Boffset%5D=10.

323. Gounley, Thomas. "25 Years After the Great Missouri Earthquake That Never Happened." BuzzFeed News. BuzzFeed News, December 5, 2015. https://www.buzzfeednews.com/article/tgounley/the-day-the-earth-stood-still.

324. "History: Fort Leonard Wood." US Army Fort Leonard Wood. United States Army. Accessed November 26, 2020. https://home.army.mil/wood/index.php/about/history.

325. "Up in the Air." IMDb. IMDb.com, December 23, 2009. https://www.imdb.com/title/tt1193138/.

326. "Treaty between the United States of America and the Union of Soviet Socialist Republics on Strategic Offensive Reductions (START I)." Nuclear Threat Initiative. Accessed January 11, 2021. https://www.nti.org/learn/treaties-and-regimes/treaties-between-united-states-america-and-union-soviet-socialist-republics-strategic-offensive-reductions-start-i-start-ii/.

327. Brown, John W. "Albert Bond Lambert: Industrialist and Aviation Pioneer." Missouri Legends. May 4, 2012. https://missourilegends.com/missouri-business-legends/albert-lambert/

328. "History of Tourism in Branson." ExploreBranson.com. City of Branson, MO, April 28, 2020. https://www.explorebranson.com/blog/history-tourism-branson-0.

329. "Joseph Pulitzer." Wikipedia. Wikimedia Foundation, December 31, 2020. https://en.wikipedia.org/wiki/Joseph_Pulitzer.

330. "Braggin' Rights." Wikipedia. Wikimedia Foundation, December 20, 2020. https://en.wikipedia.org/wiki/Braggin%27_Rights.

331. "About the Nelson-Atkins Museum of Art: History." Nelson Atkins. The Nelson-Atkins Museum of Art, December 26, 2020. https://www.nelson-atkins.org/about/.

332. "State of Missouri Et Rel. Gaines v. Canada Et Al." Legal Information Institute. Cornell University, October 26, 2020. https://www.law.cornell.edu/supremecourt/text/305/337.

333. "History of the St. Louis Cardinals (NFL)." Wikipedia. Wikimedia Foundation, January 5, 2021. https://en.wikipedia.org/wiki/History_of_the_St._Louis_Cardinals_(NFL).

334. Denney, Becky. "Causes of the Taum Sauk Reservoir Breach." Sierra Club, June 3, 2013. https://www.sierraclub.org/missouri/blog/2013/06/causes-taum-sauk-reservoir-breach#:~:text=On%20December%2014%2C%202005%2C%20the,Johnson's%20Shut%2DIns%20State%20Park.&text=The%20Taum%20Sauk%20Reservoir%20was,plant%20which%20employed%20twelve%20people.

335. "Gemini 6A." Wikipedia. Wikimedia Foundation, January 1, 2021. https://en.wikipedia.org/wiki/Gemini_6A.

336. "New Madrid Earthquakes of 1811–12." Encyclopedia Britannica. Encyclopedia Britannica, inc., December 9, 2020. https://www.britannica.com/event/New-Madrid-earthquakes-of-1811-1812.

337. Mailes, Yancy. "The B-2 Comes to Missouri." Air Force Global Strike Command. United States Air Force, December 16, 2013. https://www.afgsc.af.mil/News/Commentaries/Display/Article/629840/the-b-2-comes-to-missouri/.

338. "SEMO Community Information." Southeast Missouri State University. Accessed January 11, 2021. https://semo.edu/visitors/community.html.

339. "Callaway Nuclear Plant Fired up Three Decades Ago Today." newstribune.com. *Jefferson City News Tribune*, December 19, 2014. https://www.newstribune.com/news/news/story/2014/dec/19/watts-power-30-years-callaway-plant-nuclear/495576/.

340. "Missouri Imposed a $1 Tax on Bachelors." Old Farmer's Almanac. Accessed January 11, 2021. https://www.almanac.com/fact/missouri-imposed-a-1-tax-on-bachelors.

341. "Creve Coeur History." Creve Coeur Official Site. City of Creve Coeur, Missouri. Accessed October 11, 2020. https://www.creve-coeur.org/220/History.

342. O'Neil, Tim. "The Opening of Union Station Turned St. Louis into a National Crossroads." STLtoday.com. *St. Louis Post-Dispatch*, September 1, 2020. https://www.stltoday.com/news/archives/the-opening-of-union-station-turned-st-louis-into-a-national-crossroads/article_16d4d8d1-2490-5e82-a6a5-f0276ca33454.html.

343. Archibald, John. "Dick Weber." Encyclopedia Britannica. Encyclopedia Britannica, inc., December 19, 2020. https://www.britannica.com/biography/Dick-Weber.

344. Frankel, Todd. "Missouri Residents Recall Gasconade River Oil Spill." Columbia Missourian. Columbia Missourian, June 21, 2010. https://www.columbiamissourian.com/news/missouri-residents-recall-gasconade-river-oil-spill/article_c91cc050-820f-556e-bc98-bea2cd7b7b2a.html#:~:text=A%20massive%20pipeline%20ruptured%20on,spill%20had%20been%20largely%20forgotten.

345. Roe, Jason. "Let There Be Lights." KC History. Kansas City Public Library. Accessed September 14, 2020. https://kchistory.org/week-kansas-city-history/let-there-be-lights.

346. Lewin, Tamar. "Nancy Cruzan Dies, Outlived by a Debate Over the Right to Die." *The New York Times*. *The New York Times*, December 27, 1990. https://www.nytimes.com/1990/12/27/us/nancy-cruzan-dies-outlived-by-a-debate-over-the-right-to-die.html.

347. "Masters and Johnson." Encyclopedia Britannica. Encyclopedia Britannica, inc. Accessed December 22, 2020. https://www.britannica.com/biography/Masters-and-Johnson.

348. Inderman, Robert. "Kansas City Barbecue King Dead." UPI. United Press International, December 28, 1982. https://www.upi.com/Archives/1982/12/28/Kansas-City-barbecue-king-dead/4723409899600/.

349. "Mark Twain Lake Master Plan." Clarence Cannon Dam and Mark Twain Lake, Monroe City, MO. United States Army Corp of Engineers, 2004. https://www.mvs.usace.army.mil/portals/54/docs/recreation/marktwain/Chp1_Introduction2.pdf.

350. Sonderman, Joe. *St. Louis 365: Intriguing Events from Each Day of the Year!* St. Louis, MO: Stellar Press, 2002. p. 259

351. History Heritage of Jefferson City. City of Jefferson, MO. Accessed October 21, 2020. https://www.jeffersoncitymo.gov/live_play/history_heritage/index.php.

Index